The Early Republic and Rise of National Identity

1783–1861

Editorial Advisers

Steven A. Goldberg
Past President, National Council for the Social Studies
Social Studies Department Chair
New Rochelle High School, New Rochelle, New York

Louise A. Hazebrouck
English teacher
Horace Greeley High School, Chappaqua, New York

Deborah Boxer Minchin
Social Studies teacher
New Rochelle High School, New Rochelle, New York

HISTORY THROUGH LITERATURE
AMERICAN VOICES, AMERICAN THEMES

The Early Republic and Rise of National Identity
1783–1861

Jeffrey H. Hacker, Editor

M.E.Sharpe
Armonk, New York
London, England

Sharpe
Insights

Cover images (clockwise from top left) provided by: The Granger Collection, NYC-All rights
reserved; Buyenlarge/Getty Images; Library of Congress.

Interior Images provided by: The Granger Collection, NYC—All rights reserved, p. 4; PhotoQuest/
Getty Images, p. 19; The Granger Collection, NYC—All rights reserved, p. 36; Buyenlarge/Getty
Images, p. 50; Library of Congress, p. 54; The Granger Collection, NYC—All rights reserved,
p. 65; Library of Congress, p. 72; The Granger Collection, NYC—All rights reserved, p. 92;
Hulton Archive/Getty Images, p. 111; Hulton Archive/Getty Images, p. 123; MPI/Getty Images,
p. 137; The Granger Collection, NYC—All rights reserved, p. 154; Library of Congress, p. 161;
Library of Congress, p. 182.

The EuroSlavic fonts used to create this work are © 1986–2013 Payne Loving Trust.
EuroSlavic is available from Linguist's Software, Inc.,
www.linguistsoftware.com, P.O. Box 580, Edmonds, WA 98020-0580 USA
tel (425) 775-1130.

Library of Congress Cataloging-in-Publication Data

The early republic and rise of national identity, 1783-1861 / Jeffrey H. Hacker, Editor.
    pages cm.—(History through literature : American voices, American themes) (Sharpe
insights)
    Includes bibliographical references and index.
    ISBN 978-0-7656-8340-3 (cloth : alk. paper) — ISBN 978-0-7656-8322-9 (pbk. : alk. paper)
    ISBN 978-0-7656-8323-6 (electronic)
    1. Literature and history—United States—History—19th century. 2. National characteristics,
American, in literature. 3. American literature—19th century. I. Hacker, Jeffrey H., editor of
compilation.

PS169.H5E27 2014
810.9′358—dc23 2013010945

Printed in the United States of America

The paper used in this publication meets the minimum requirements of
American National Standard for Information Sciences
Permanence of Paper for Printed Library Materials,
ANSI Z 39.48-1984.

IBT (c)   10   9   8   7   6   5   4   3   2   1
IBT (p)   10   9   8   7   6   5   4   3   2   1

Contents

Preface

History Through Literature: The Early Republic and Rise of National Identity (1783–1861) is the second in a six-volume series designed to support interdisciplinary coursework and independent reading in American history and letters. The material presented in each volume is selected and organized to enrich the study of the nation's historical record, its literary heritage, and their mutual influences.

Each volume begins with a chronology that identifies, defines, and places in context the notable historical events, literary works, authors' lives, and cultural movements of the period in question. The centerpiece of the volume is a comprehensive overview essay that highlights the era's major historical trends, social and cultural movements, literary voices, and landmark works as reflections of each other and the spirit of the times. The core content comprises some 20–30 shorter articles—all drawn from the archives of the Sharpe Reference and Sharpe Online Reference imprints—on lives and works in period literature, including extended excerpts. Special features called *Sidelights* apply a different lens to this exploration, focusing on historical literature as a reflection of both the time of the actual events and the time of the writing. In the present volume, for example, *Sidelights* consider early American history writing and satires inspired by Transcendentalist utopian communities.

Throughout the series, the designation of historical and literary "periods" is not bound by strict start–end dates or specific events (with such key exceptions as national independence, the Civil War, the Great Depression, and World War II). The lives and works of writers obviously overlap any arbitrarily defined eras, and their styles and themes often evolve in ways that defy neat historical classification. Thus, the designation of historical periods and the selection of subjects in each volume are guided by subjective judgments based on a confluence of factors—historical events, social and economic trends, and the rise and decline of artistic and cultural movements.

This volume—simply enough, it would seem—begins with the formal conclusion of the Revolutionary War (Treaty of Paris, September 1783) and ends with the first cannon fire of the Civil War (Fort Sumter, April 1861). Clearly, however, major historical and literary themes of this period are not easily separated from those of the war years themselves or the Reconstruction era that followed. The defining events and issues of antebellum America—slavery, abolitionism, and the failure to reach an enduring regional compromise—are surely of a piece with those of 1861 and beyond; they are most usefully studied together.

Thus, taking a thematic rather than strictly chronological approach, this volume focuses less on the literature of slavery and abolition (leaving that to the next volume in the series) and is organized around the rise of a distinctive national identity and literary tradition. While giving due recognition to the emergence of the slave narrative as a literary form and to the influence of Harriet Beecher Stowe's *Uncle Tom's Cabin* on the events and tenor of the times, for example, the articles and excerpts in this volume emphasize a different theme: the birth and infancy of American literature independent of British culture, with a unique voice and perspective, both shaping and shaped by the task of establishing the new nation.

Careful readers will rightly observe that this did not occur in a moment or a decade or even a half-century, but that it evolved in phases and stages over the course of the entire 78-year span. The immediate post–Revolutionary years naturally placed a high priority on such practical concerns as establishing a viable government, economy, and way of life independent of Britain. As even Benjamin Franklin put it, "To America, one schoolmaster is worth a dozen poets, and the invention of a machine or the improvement of an implement is of more importance than a masterpiece. . . ."

William Brown Hill's novel *The Power of Sympathy,* said to be the first written by an American on American soil, was published in 1789, the year of George Washington's inauguration as the first U.S. president. In the aftermath of the War of 1812, with the young nation on more secure footing, Washington Irving and James Fenimore Cooper became the first American writers to win widespread acclaim in Europe—the former with such short stories as "The Legend of Sleepy Hollow" and "Rip Van Winkle," the latter with his series of novels called the Leatherstocking Tales, all of them uniquely American in setting, sensibility, and style.

The 1830s gave rise to a new philosophical, literary, and social movement with a distinctly American character—Transcendentalism. Forged by the likes of Ralph Waldo Emerson, Henry David Thoreau, Margaret Fuller, and their circle of friends, former clergymen, educators, and thinkers in New England, the movement sought nothing less than a new relationship between humanity and the universe, embracing nature, the human imagination, and the inner spiritual world over organized religion, the dictates of society, or material well-being.

Noting as well the contributions of the Fireside Poets (William Cullen Bryant, Oliver Wendell Holmes, Henry Wadsworth Longfellow, James Russell Lowell, and John Greenleaf Whittier), the Gothic short-story writer and poet Edgar Allan Poe, and other literary lights—all represented in the pages that follow—modern literary critics have pointed to the period from about 1830 to 1861 as the "American Renaissance" in literature. In a groundbreaking work of literary criticism (*American Renaissance*, 1941), F.O. Matthiessen focuses on the five-year period 1850–1855 as the high point of that literary flowering. Remarkably, that short span of years produced such classics as Nathaniel Hawthorne's *The Scarlet Letter* (1850) and *The House of the Seven Gables* (1851), Herman Melville's *Moby-Dick* (1851), Thoreau's *Walden* (1854), and Walt Whitman's first edition of *Leaves of Grass* (1855), not to mention Emerson's essay collection *Representative Men* (1850), Stowe's *Uncle Tom's Cabin* (1852), and Longfellow's "Song of Hiawatha" (1855), among others.

Inevitably, enduring works of literature such as these stand as vital documents of political, social, intellectual, and cultural history no less than as products of individual creative inspiration. The authors and works presented in this volume, practitioners and prominent examples of prose fiction, poetry, social commentary, and history, offer compelling case studies in the study of both history through literature and literature through history.

Chronology

1783   The Treaty of Paris, signed on September 3, marks the official end of the Revolutionary War and the formal recognition of the United States as a sovereign nation.

1788   The U.S. Constitution is officially ratified on June 21, as New Hampshire becomes the ninth of the 13 colonies to vote in favor of ratification.

1789   The new federal government begins operation on March 4; George Washington is sworn in as the first president on April 30.

William Hill Brown publishes *The Power of Sympathy*, generally recognized as the first American novel—that is, the first written by an American on American soil. A sentimental novel in epistolary form, it is dedicated to the "Young Ladies of United Columbia."

The Interesting Narrative of the Life of Olaudah Equiano gives readers a firsthand account of the capture of a native African boy, his transport to America as a slave, his eventual freedom, and his role in the abolitionist movement. The highly popular autobiography is the first notable work in the slave narrative genre.

1791   William Bartram writes *Travels Through North and South Carolina, Georgia, East and West Florida*. One of the earliest American travelogues, it is among the first works to detail the unique characteristics of the American countryside.

1798   Charles Brockden Brown, America's first professional author, begins his career with two Gothic novels, *Alcuin: A Dialogue* and *Wieland; or, The Transformation*. Within a year, three more of his novels will follow: *Ormond; or The Secret Witness*, *Arthur Mervyn*, and *Edgar Huntly*. The last of these is the first mystery novel set in the United States.

1800   Mason Locke Weems publishes his *Life of Washington*. Although the book is more fiction than fact, it is wildly popular and exerts an enduring influence on the national mythology.

        The Library of Congress is founded in Washington, D.C. Created to provide "such books as may be necessary for the use of Congress," the collection will grow to become the national library of the United States.

1803   The Louisiana Purchase doubles the area of the United States with the acquisition of 828,000 square miles of territory from France. The following year, Meriwether Lewis and William Clark begin their two-year voyage of exploration—and a richly detailed journal that describes the land, wildlife, and peoples of the American West for the first time.

1809   Washington Irving pens the best-selling work of humor *Diedrich Knickerbocker's History of New York*. His first literary success, the book makes Irving a celebrity in Europe as well as the United States.

1812–14 Following repeated violations of its neutrality, the United States declares war on Britain on June 18. Before the official end of the fighting in December 1814, U.S. forces invade Canada twice and the British set fire to Washington, D.C. The United States emerges from the War of 1812 on more solid footing; a wave of nationalism sweeps the republic.

        The Walnut Street Theatre, today America's oldest, is founded in Philadelphia.

1817   William Cullen Bryant publishes his landmark poem "Thanatopsis," a meditation on death and nature. Other prominent works on the theme of nature, including "To a Waterfowl" (1821), "A Forest Hymn" (1825), and "The Prairies" (1833), will follow.

1819–20 Washington Irving publishes his most famous work, *The Sketch Book of Geoffrey Crayon, Gent.* The collection contains the two short stories for which Irving is most remembered: "Rip Van Winkle" and "The Legend of Sleepy Hollow."

1823   James Fenimore Cooper publishes *The Pioneers*, the first of his Leatherstocking Tales, a series of frontier adventures featuring the character Natty Bumppo. The highly successful series ultimately will include *The Last of the Mohicans* (1826), *The Prairie* (1827), *The Pathfinder* (1840), and *The Deerslayer* (1841).

1828   Noah Webster publishes his magnum opus, the *American Dictionary of the English Language.* The book gives shape to a uniquely American form of English.

1829   *Metamora; or, Last of the Wampanoags,* one of the first plays to feature Native American characters, is a runaway success.

1834   George Bancroft publishes his *History of the United States from the Discovery of the American Continent,* covering the period 1492–1660. Nine more volumes, which continue the narrative through the Civil War, will follow by 1874. For this body of work, Bancroft will be recognized as the first American historian of note.

1836   Amos Bronson Alcott, Orestes Brownson, William Ellery Channing, Ralph Waldo Emerson, Margaret Fuller, Theodore Parker, George Ripley, and others form the Transcendental Club in Cambridge, Massachusetts. From the group emerges the philosophical, literary, and social movement of Transcendentalism.

1837   Emerson delivers an address at Harvard University titled "An American Scholar," in which he calls on the nation's academic and literary communities to throw off European influences and forge a uniquely American intellectual tradition. Poet, essayist, and physician Oliver Wendell Holmes will refer to Emerson's address as America's "Intellectual Declaration of Independence."

1839   Edgar Allan Poe publishes "The Fall of the House of Usher," the first in his series of classic Gothic short stories. It will be followed by "The Murders in the Rue Morgue" (1841), "The Pit and the Pendulum" (1842), and "The Tell-Tale Heart" (1843).

1840   *The Dial*, the leading journal of the Transcendentalist movement, is founded in Boston. Edited by Margaret Fuller and then Ralph Waldo Emerson, the magazine publishes articles by the brightest lights of the movement but closes, owing to financial difficulties, within four years.

1846   Herman Melville launches his literary career with *Typee: A Peep at Polynesian Life*; its sequel, *Omoo*, will follow a year later. Both works are based on his experiences in the South Pacific, and both win wide acclaim.

1846–48 The Mexican-American War breaks out in April 1846 and continues until February 1848. The final peace treaty cedes California and the present-day states of the Southwest to the United States and recognizes the U.S. annexation of Texas.

1847   Zane Carroll Judson, using the pseudonym "Ned Buntline," publishes his first two dime novels: *The Last Days of Calleo; or the Doomed City of Sin*, and *The King of the Sea: A Tale of the Fearless and Free*. Buntline will become the most successful practitioner of that wildly popular genre.

1848   James Russell Lowell publishes the first series of *The Biglow Papers*, a popular satire on slavery and the Mexican-

American War. It is notable as one of the first major literary works to employ American vernacular speech.

1849   Henry David Thoreau publishes an essay titled "Resistance to Civil Government"—later "Civil Disobedience"—in which he argues that an individual's conscience must take priority over civil law, justifying disobedience on grounds of moral principle. The essay began as a lecture explaining Thoreau's refusal to pay his poll tax—and willingness to go to jail—to protest slavery and the Mexican-American War in 1846. His argument would have a direct effect on the nonviolent resistance campaigns by Mohandas Gandhi, Martin Luther King, Jr., and others in the twentieth century.

Working-class fans of actor Edwin Forrest clash with the upper-class fans of actor William Charles Macready in the Astor Place Riot. The incident in New York City, which leaves 20 people dead, is the deadliest outbreak of urban violence to that point in U.S. history.

1850   Congress passes a series of laws, collectively known as the Compromise of 1850, that seeks to end the sectional dispute over slavery. In reality, the compromise will serve only to postpone the escalation of the conflict, if not destabilize the nation even further.

Quaker poet John Greenleaf Whittier, one of the era's most prominent men of letters, publishes "Ichabod," a virulently antislavery poem in response to Senator Daniel Webster's defection from the abolitionist cause to support the Compromise of 1850.

Nathaniel Hawthorne publishes *The Scarlet Letter*, a meditation on Puritan faith, sin, and redemption that will become one of the classics of American literature. The novel will be followed the next year by Hawthorne's *The House of the Seven Gables*.

1851   Herman Melville publishes *Moby-Dick*. The tale of Captain Ahab and his maniacal quest for revenge against a great white whale earns tepid reviews and meager sales. The novel is not recognized as a masterpiece of American Romanticism until long after Melville's death.

1852   Harriet Beecher Stowe publishes *Uncle Tom's Cabin; or, Life Among the Lowly*, a biting critique of slavery and the best-selling work of American literature in the nineteenth century.

1854   Henry David Thoreau publishes *Walden*, a narrative of his two-year experiment in simple living in the woods of Massachusetts. One of the essential texts of the Transcendentalist movement, *Walden* will have a profound effect on nature writing and counterculture movements in America for generations to come.

William Gilmore Simms assumes the editorship of the Charleston, South Carolina–based *Southern Quarterly Review*, which establishes him as the leading literary figure of the antebellum South.

The first public library in the United States opens in Boston.

1855   Walt Whitman publishes the first edition of *Leaves of Grass*, consisting of 12 poems. The volume is not well received, but Whitman will revise and expand the collection in eight subsequent editions (the last in 1892). *Leaves of Grass* will become one of the icons of nineteenth-century American literature.

Henry Wadsworth Longfellow produces his epic poem *The Song of Hiawatha*, recounting the birth, life, romance, and death of an Ojibwa Indian prophet and drawing extensively on native legend and folklore.

1861   The January issue of *Atlantic Monthly* carries Henry Wadsworth Longfellow's best-known poem, "Paul Revere's

Ride," a look back at the start of the American Revolution on the eve of the Civil War.

On April 12, following declarations of secession by seven Southern states in the previous months, Confederate cannons open fire on the federal garrison of Fort Sumter, South Carolina. Four years of civil war ensue.

Literature of the Early Republic

Literature in all its forms—from novels, short stories, plays, and poetry to sermons, essays, political tracts, and histories—played a formative role in the early decades of the republic, helping Americans imagine their nation into being and establishing a national identity. American writers from independence to the Civil War forged a tradition of native, national literature independent of British culture, even as American readers continued to consume works produced in Great Britain and elsewhere in Europe.

Intersecting with a number of social, cultural, economic, and political movements—ranging from Enlightenment philosophy and European Romanticism to debates over abolition and westward expansion—American literature of the period both shaped and was shaped by the task of establishing a new nation. The intimate relationship between literature and the republic is reflected in the often-used modern label "Great American Novel"—a designation that presupposes the best American literature develops a distinctively American voice, capturing the "spirit" of the country.

Influence of British Writing

Prior to the nineteenth century, people in North America primarily read novels written in Europe. Many of these novels, particularly sentimental fiction written by such British authors as Samuel Richardson, were adapted and edited for American audiences. In the early years of the United States, which saw a rise in literacy and a corresponding increase in the popularity of fiction, the majority of novel readers were women. Tales of seduction, stories of sympathy, and, more generally, any plot involving courtship and marriage were especially popular.

1

A good example of these trends can be found in the title that many scholars consider the first American novel—that is, the first written by an American on American soil. William Hill Brown's *The Power of Sympathy* was published in 1789, the same year George Washington was inaugurated as the first president of the United States. Billed as an educational novel dedicated to the "Young Ladies of United Columbia," *The Power of Sympathy* was the subject of an intensive advertising campaign. An ad in the journal *Herald of Freedom*, for instance, was tagged with the headline "An *American* Novel." The emphasis "American" underscores the extent to which the novel's publishers sought to promote the book as the first of its kind: a distinctly American novel written in and for the new nation. In reality, they overstated the case, as the novel draws on a number of literary conventions popular in England: It is written as a correspondence, like Samuel Richardson's popular epistolary novels of the 1740s and 1750s, and features a plot that turns on seduction, family secrets, illegitimate children, and sympathy—all popular themes of British novels during that era.

> American writers from independence to the Civil War forged a tradition of native, national literature independent of British culture.

Another trend in European, and specifically English, literature that strongly influenced early American fiction writers was the emergence of Gothic tales. Surviving to this day in the genre of popular literature known as horror fiction, the Gothic tale experienced a surge of popularity in Britain during the last decades of the eighteenth century. Set in remote locations, these tales featured an array of recognizable conventions: spooky castles, morally questionable aristocrats, curses, ghosts, damsels in distress, and madness. In the United States, the first important Gothic author was Charles Brockden Brown. Born into a Quaker family in 1771, Brown originally trained to be a lawyer, but his interest in literature took over his career by the 1790s. He was influenced by both the French Revolution and the work of radical British writers such as Mary Wollstonecraft, author of the famous *A Vindication of the Rights of Women* (1792). With such novels as *Wieland* (1798) and *Arthur Mervyn* (1799), Brown helped popularize the Gothic genre in the United States. He, in turn, influenced British writers such as Mary Shelley—the daughter of Wollstonecraft and the author of *Frankenstein* (1818)—as well as American writers such as Nathaniel Hawthorne, Herman Melville, and Edgar Allan Poe. Poe's Gothic works are especially well remembered, as he became a master of the genre. His short stories "The Fall of the House of Usher" (1839), "The Murders in the Rue Morgue" (1841), "The Pit and the Pendulum" (1842), and "The Tell-Tale Heart" (1843) are still widely read today.

Rise of a National Tradition

At the beginning of the nineteenth century, a new generation of American short-story and novel writers appeared on the scene. As the War of 1812 was cementing independence, writers began to create a native tradition of distinctly American literature. Among these new voices, perhaps the two best known and most influential were Washington Irving and James Fenimore Cooper, who became the first American authors to experience widespread popularity in Europe.

Born in 1783 in New York City, Washington Irving was a voracious reader of English literature as a child, enjoying works by Joseph Addison, Oliver Goldsmith, William Shakespeare, and Laurence Sterne. In 1808, Irving began work on his parody *Diedrich Knickerbocker's History of New York* (1809), which introduced the term "Knickerbocker" into American slang; the word's association with New York society persists to the present day. The book was Irving's first great success, bringing him a measure of celebrity in the United States and Europe. Ten years later, Irving followed with *The Sketch Book of Geoffrey Crayon, Gent.* (1819–1820), which contains the short stories for which Irving is best remembered, "The Legend of Sleepy Hollow" and "Rip Van Winkle." Set in New York's Hudson River valley during the years immediately following the American Revolution, "The Legend of Sleepy Hollow" features the schoolmaster Ichabod Crane, who is pursued by the Headless Horseman—identified as the ghost of a Revolutionary War soldier who lost his head in battle. "Rip Van Winkle," meanwhile, tells the story of a Dutch American settler who falls asleep in the Catskill Mountains and wakes up 20 years later to discover that the American Revolution has taken place. In addition to these distinctly American works, Irving produced a number of novels, travel books, histories, and biographies.

Washington Irving (seated center, legs crossed), America's first internationally renowned author, is joined by Hawthorne, Emerson, Cooper, and other contemporaries at his estate in Tarrytown, New York.

James Fenimore Cooper, born in 1789 in Burlington, New Jersey, was taken at a young age to the residence of his wealthy and influential father on Otsego Lake in central New York. After being expelled from school in Albany, Cooper became a sailor and eventually joined the navy. After inheriting his father's fortune, he married Susan De Lancey and settled in upstate New York. Established in his new circumstances, he wrote and published two novels: *Precaution* (1820), a novel of manners set in the society of English aristocrats, and *The Spy* (1821), a romance about the American Revolution.

In 1823, after moving to New York City, Cooper began publishing his Leatherstocking Tales, a series of novels about the adventures of the fictional frontiersman Natty Bumppo. Undoubtedly influenced by Cooper's own childhood experiences on the New York frontier, the Leatherstocking Tales explore the intersection of European American and Native American cultures. The most famous of these novels is *The Last of the Mohicans* (1826), set during the French and Indian War of 1754–1763. Although the novel takes place in the relatively distant past, *The Last of the Mohicans* clearly references debates over

Native American culture that were current in Cooper's time. Beginning with the Thomas Jefferson administration, the U.S. government had adopted policies that encouraged the assimilation of Native Americans into European American culture. *The Last of the Mohicans*, like the other Leatherstocking Tales, depicts the reverse process: a frontiersman who assimilates into native ways of life, straddling the divide between the two cultures.

Overall, the American settings, Romantic themes, and bold tones of Irving's and Cooper's works directly influenced the fiction of the authors who wrote after them: Nathaniel Hawthorne's colonial romances, Henry Wadsworth Longfellow's epic ballads, and Herman Melville's sea adventures. It was Irving, in fact, who encouraged the publishing house of George P. Putnam to print an American edition of Melville's first book, the South Pacific adventure *Typee* (1846). Literary critics of the time began to identify the emergence of a distinctly American tradition. According to a British review of Melville's *Moby-Dick* (1851),

> *Edgar Poe, Nathaniel Hawthorne, Herman Melville are assuredly no British offshoots; nor is Emerson—the German American that he is! The observer of this commencement of an American literature, properly so called, will notice as significant that these writers have a wild and mystic love of the supersensual, peculiarly their own.*

Social and Political Themes

As fiction writers of the early nineteenth century were writing Romantic tales of the sea, the West, and the colonial past, American literature intersected with a number of other contemporary intellectual and political currents, particularly in the Mid-Atlantic states and New England. Prominent among these was the movement known as Transcendentalism, promoted by a group of New England writers that included Ralph Waldo Emerson, Margaret Fuller, George Putnam, and Henry David Thoreau. Although these writers, intellectuals, and activists primarily wrote essays and poetry, their celebration of the natural world both influenced and was influenced by the novels of the period.

The progressive political views of the Transcendentalists were also highly influential. On April 23, 1838, Emerson wrote a letter to President Martin Van Buren decrying the forced migration of the Cherokee Nation. In the letter, Emerson asked "whether all the attributes of reason, of civility, of justice, and even of mercy, shall be put off by the American people, and so vast an outrage upon the Cherokee Nation and upon human nature shall be consummated." In 1845, Fuller addressed the topic of women's independence in *Woman in the Nineteenth Century*, one of the first feminist texts published in the United States.

It was slavery and abolition, however, that most sparked the writers of both fiction and nonfiction during this period. Thoreau, like other Transcendentalists, was a committed abolitionist who delivered lectures and wrote essays that condemned the institution of slavery. Melville referred to the enslavement of Africans as "man's foulest crime" and took up the subject in his short story "Benito Cereno" (1856), about a slave rebellion aboard a Spanish ship. Slavery and abolition were also thematic concerns in the writings of poet and essayist Walt Whitman before and during the Civil War.

The subject of slavery was not the exclusive province of white intellectuals, to be sure. Among the notable literary developments in antebellum America was the emergence of slave narratives— autobiographical accounts of slave life—as an important genre. Prominent examples include *The Interesting Narrative of the Life of Olaudah Equiano* (1789), *The History of Mary Prince, A West Indian Slave* (1831), and *Incidents in the Life of a Slave Girl* (1861) by Harriet Jacobs. Preeminent among works in this genre is the autobiography of the former slave and committed abolitionist, *Narrative of the Life of Frederick Douglass, an American Slave* (1845). The book tells the story of his life from early childhood as a slave in Maryland until his escape to Massachusetts in 1838 at the age of 20.

The stir created by the publication of Douglass's *Narrative* was exceeded only by that surrounding Harriet Beecher Stowe's novel *Uncle Tom's Cabin* (1852). Born into a deeply religious Connecticut family, Stowe spent her childhood in New England and relocated with her family to Cincinnati, Ohio, where for 18 years she lived just across the Ohio River from slaves and slave owners in Kentucky. Inspired by abolitionist sentiment, Stowe began publishing *Uncle Tom's Cabin* in serial installments on June 5, 1851, in the journal *National Era*. When the novel was published in its entirety less than a year later, it became an instant success, selling about 350,000 copies in the first year alone. It became the second-best-selling book of the nineteenth century in the United States, exceeded by only the Bible.

Although many have criticized the novel for its perpetuation of black stereotypes, *Uncle Tom's Cabin* made a dramatic contribution to the national debate over slavery in the years leading up to the Civil War. Its social and political realism marked a departure from the romance adventures that had dominated the American literary scene until then. In this respect, *Uncle Tom's Cabin* set the tone for the dominant trends of the nation's literature in the aftermath of the Civil War and into the twentieth century. Its influence can be detected in later works as diverse as Mark Twain's *Adventures of Huckleberry Finn* (1885), Stephen Crane's *The Red Badge of Courage* (1895), and Upton Sinclair's *The Jungle* (1906), to name only a few. All of these books would continue the job that American writers did so much to accomplish in the antebellum era—creating a uniquely American style of literature.

Corey McEleney

See also: Environment and Nature, Views of; Libraries and Lyceums; Poetry; Theater; Transcendentalism

◇◇◇

Sidelight

Writing Early American History

The founding of the United States as a sovereign nation marked the genesis not only of U.S. history but also of U.S. historiography (the writing of history). In the decades following independence, the nation's historians focused their attention on the American Revolution and Constitution. The first serious works tended to take views that corresponded with the competing political ideologies of the new republic—Federalism and Republicanism.

Among the earliest histories of the war of independence was the three-volume *History of the Rise, Progress, and Termination of the American Revolution* (1805), by Massachusetts playwright, poet, and patriot Mercy Otis Warren. In the florid, Manichean (good vs. evil) style of the times, the book reflected her anti-

Federalist, Jeffersonian philosophy. A consolidated central government, in Warren's view, tends toward despotism and the abridgement of natural rights unless opposed by reason. Thus, her account of the revolution emphasized the eternal battle between popular liberty and the dangers of arbitrary, unrepresentative government.

In contrast to Warren's *History* stands the five-volume *Life of George Washington* (1804–1807), by Chief Justice John Marshall. An authorized biography in the sense that Marshall made use of extensive records and papers provided by Washington's family, the work went much further than a life story, providing a comprehensive political and military history of the Revolutionary era. As a longtime leader of the Federal Party and political rival of Thomas Jefferson, Marshall brought a clear Federalist perspective to his study. In extolling Washington's greatness as a general and president, he emphasized the deeds that helped create a strong self-governing country out of a tenuous union of states. In more overtly political terms, he defended the policies of the Washington administration against the criticisms of Republican opponents. Regardless of its biases, historians hold Marshall's work in high esteem for its accuracy, detail, and comprehensiveness.

The sheer authority of Marshall's *Life of George Washington* came as an answer to what was then—and remains today—the best-known biography of the first president, Mason Locke Weems's fanciful *Life of Washington.* Rushed to publication months after Washington's death, Weems's lively and engaging book proved enormously popular and went through numerous printings. But it could hardly be called history. More interested in moralizing and creating an American icon than in documenting facts, Weems simply invented much of his account. His contributions to the national mythology include the famous tale about young George and his father's cherry tree:

> When George . . . was about six years old, he was made the
> wealthy master of a hatchet! of which, like most little boys,
> he was immoderately fond, and was constantly going about
> chopping everything that came in his way. One day, in the

garden, where he often amused himself hacking his mother's pea-sticks, he unluckily tried the edge of his hatchet on the body of a beautiful young English cherry-tree, which he barked so terribly, that I don't believe the tree ever got the better of it. The next morning the old gentleman, finding out what had befallen his tree, which, by the by, was a great favourite, came into the house; and with much warmth asked for the mischievous author, declaring at the same time, that he would not have taken five guineas for his tree. Nobody could tell him anything about it. Presently George and his hatchet made their appearance. "George," said his father, "do you know who killed that beautiful little cherry tree yonder in the garden?" This was a tough question; and George staggered under it for a moment; but quickly recovered himself: and looking at his father, with the sweet face of youth brightened with the inexpressible charm of all-conquering truth, he bravely cried out, "I can't tell a lie, Pa; you know I can't tell a lie. I did cut it with my hatchet."—"Run to my arms, you dearest boy," cried his father in transports, "run to my arms; glad am I, George, that you killed my tree; for you have paid me for it a thousand fold. Such an act of heroism in my son is more worth than a thousand trees, though blossomed with silver, and their fruits of purest gold."

Serious histories in succeeding decades continued to reflect the split in political ideology. In his three-volume *History of the United States* (1816–1817), the conservative South Carolinian David Ramsay explicitly advocated republican values in reforming American society but called for the preservation of existing institutions. Conversely, Richard Hildreth of Massachusetts took a Federalist, anti-Jeffersonian stance in his meticulous, highly factual six-volume *History of the United States* (1849–1852).

Hildreth's dry tomes gave way to the more compelling, scholarly, and highly popular narratives of George Bancroft, generally acknowledged as the preeminent historian of the early United States. A diplomat and politician (who, as secretary of the navy, established the U.S. Naval Academy at Annapolis), Bancroft earned a reputation as "the father of American history" for his 10-volume *History of the United States from the Discovery of the American Continent* (1834–1874), covering the colonial period to 1782. His two-volume *History of the Formation of the Constitution of the United States of America* (1882) extended the narrative to 1789.

Romantic in style, often sentimental in tone, and baldly patriotic in message, Bancroft's sweeping account faced criticism from later generations of "objective" historians. Nevertheless, Bancroft has remained esteemed in the community of scholars for setting new standards in historical research and for elevating historiography to a higher plane. His purpose was not to write "objective" history but to demonstrate how broad truths shape and move the world in its proper direction. The task of the true historian, Bancroft wrote, is to faithfully apply "inductive methods to the pursuit of history." In doing so, he explained, the historian lays bare the truth "that humanity is steadily advancing." In particular, he regarded the United States as a nation inspired and directed by God. Although modern historians reject this approach, Bancroft's vast body of research and analysis stands as a landmark of American historiography.

Bryant, William Cullen

(1794–1878)

A Massachusetts-born poet, political writer, and journalist, William Cullen Bryant edited the *New-York Evening Post* for 50 years (1828–1878). In that capacity, he wielded enormous influence as a political commentator, poet, essayist, and booster for the development of New York City. Bryant's poetry, which made him famous throughout America and England, embodied the defining elements of the Romantic movement: a veneration of nature, a deep appreciation of the beautiful and the sublime, a fixation on mortality, and the adulation of great men and heroes. Bryant is also counted among the Fireside Poets, a group of popular nineteenth-century New England verse-makers that also included Oliver Wendell Holmes, Henry Wadsworth Longfellow, James Russell Lowell, and John Greenleaf Whittier; Bryant was the first to gain a wide following.

He was born on November 3, 1794, in Cummington, Massachusetts, to Peter Bryant, a doctor and politician, and Sarah Snell Cooper. As a youth, Bryant demonstrated a formidable literary talent with his verse satire on the Thomas Jefferson administration, *The Embargo; or, Sketches of the Times*, which appeared in print in 1808. The poem became wildly popular, in part because of its reference to Jefferson's affair with his slave, Sally Hemings: "Go scan, philosophist, thy Sally's charms / And sink supinely in her sable arms."

Not long thereafter, Bryant began work on "Thanatopsis," what would become his most famous poem. A meditation on death inspired by classical Greek literature, "Thanatopsis" was revised over the course of several years and submitted to the *North American Review* in 1817. The magazine's editor initially was skeptical of Bryant's authorship, asserting, "No one, on this side of the Atlantic, is capable of writing such verses." His concerns ultimately were assuaged, and the poem was published later that year.

Despite a prolific output, Bryant earned little money from his poems and was compelled to work to support his art. He spent a brief time at Williams College, then left to pursue a legal career. After being admitted to the bar in 1815, he practiced law in western Massachusetts for a decade. In 1821, he married Francis Fairchild; they had two daughters.

Bryant's law practice was not successful enough to allow him to support his family, and, even if it had been, he grew to hate the profession. In search of a new career, Bryant and the family moved to New York City in 1825, where he worked as a writer for several short-lived newspapers. By 1828, he had become part-owner and editor of the *New-York Evening Post*, which he would edit for the rest of his life.

When he took over the *Post*, Bryant and the newspaper both stood squarely behind Andrew Jackson and the Democratic Party. Over the course of the next 30 years, however, Bryant would become disenchanted with the Democrats. He was frustrated by the annexation of Texas in 1845 and by other concessions to the South, particularly the Kansas-Nebraska Act of 1854. Two years later, when Massachusetts senator Charles Sumner was attacked by South Carolina representative Preston Brooks on the floor of the Senate for delivering an address criticizing efforts to spread slavery, Bryant wrote, "Are we [Northerners] too, slaves, slaves for life, a target for their brutal blows . . . ?"

In the election of 1856, Bryant supported John C. Frémont and the Republican Party, an expression of his mounting frustration with Southern control of the federal government. In 1859, when abolitionist fanatic John Brown was executed for his attack on the federal arsenal at Harpers Ferry, Virginia, Bryant declared him a "martyr." As a leading editor and spokesman for unhappy Democrats, Bryant channeled disaffected voters away from the party into new Northern organizations such as the Free Soil movement and the Republican Party. He also played an important role in securing the critical state of New York for Abraham Lincoln in 1860 and 1864.

Bryant remained a prolific writer and poet throughout his years as editor of the *Post*. Published works include *Tales of Glauber-Spa*

(1832); *Fountain and Other Poems* (1842); *The White Footed Deer and Other Poems* (1844); *Letters of a Traveler* (1859), a memoir of his extensive travels through Europe; *Thirty Poems* (1864); translations of Homer's *Iliad* (1870) and *Odyssey* (1871); and the first volumes of the *Popular History of the United States* (1876). After his death, a New York publisher released the complete *Life and Works of William Cullen Bryant* in six volumes (1880).

Besides his writing, Bryant invested considerable energy in service to New York City, where he was a key supporter of the creation of Central Park and the Metropolitan Museum of Art. He did much to help develop local artistic talent and aided in the emergence of the Hudson River School of painting. He also championed immigrants' rights and supported the city's labor unions.

Bryant remained energetic to the end of his life, dying on June 12, 1878, of complications from an accidental fall after giving a speech in Central Park. His son-in-law, Parke Goodwin, assumed the editorship of the *Post.* In the history of American letters, Bryant is known as one of the early advocates and practitioners of a national literary tradition.

Nicholas Cox

See also: Environment and Nature, Views of; Poetry

◇◇

"Thanatopsis," 1817

◇◇

William Cullen Bryant was one of America's first great poets. "Thanatopsis"—penned when he was only 17 years old and published in the North American Review *several years later—remains his best-known and most highly regarded work. The title of the poem translates roughly as "Meditation on Death"; human mortality was a central concern of nineteenth-century Romantic poetry. Bryant's verse also reflects a keen interest in nature, another theme that would be repeated in the defining cultural expressions of the period, including the books and essays of the Transcendentalists and the paintings of the Hudson River School, among others.*

To him who in the love of Nature holds
Communion with her visible forms, she speaks
A various language; for his gayer hours
She has a voice of gladness, and a smile
And eloquence of beauty, and she glides
Into his darker musings, with a mild
And healing sympathy, that steals away
Their sharpness, ere he is aware. When thoughts
Of the last bitter hour come like a blight
Over thy spirit, and sad images
Of the stern agony, and shroud, and pall,
And breathless darkness, and the narrow house,
Make thee to shudder and grow sick at heart;—
Go forth, under the open sky, and list
To Nature's teachings, while from all around—
Earth and her waters, and the depths of air;—
Comes a still voice—Yet a few days, and thee
The all-beholding sun shall see no more
In all his course; nor yet in the cold ground,
Where thy pale form was laid with many tears,
Nor in the embrace of ocean, shall exist
Thy image. Earth, that nourished thee, shall claim
Thy growth, to be resolved to earth again,
And, lost each human trace, surrendering up
Thine individual being, shalt thou go
To mix for ever with the elements,
To be a brother to the insensible rock
And to the sluggish clod, which the rude swain
Turns with his share, and treads upon. The oak
Shall send his roots abroad, and pierce thy mould.
Yet not to thine eternal resting-place
Shalt thou retire alone—nor couldst thou wish
Couch more magnificent. Thou shalt lie down
With patriarchs of the infant world—with kings,
The powerful of the earth—the wise, the good,
Fair forms, and hoary seers of ages past,

All in one mighty sepulchre.—The hills
Rock-ribb'd and ancient as the sun,—the vales
Stretching in pensive quietness between;
The venerable woods—rivers that move
In majesty, and the complaining brooks
That make the meadows green; and, poured round all,
Old Ocean's grey and melancholy waste,—
Are but the solemn decorations all
Of the great tomb of man. The golden sun,
The planets, all the infinite host of heaven,
Are shining on the sad abodes of death,
Through the still lapse of ages. All that tread
The globe are but a handful to the tribes
That slumber in its bosom.—Take the wings
Of morning—and the Barcan desert pierce,
Or lose thyself in the continuous woods
Where rolls the Oregon, and hears no sound,
Save his own dashings—yet—the dead are there;
And millions in those solitudes, since first
The flight of years began, have laid them down
In their last sleep—the dead reign there alone.
So shalt thou rest—and what if thou withdraw
In silence from the living—and no friend
Take note of thy departure? All that breathe
Will share thy destiny. The gay will laugh
When thou art gone, the solemn brood of care
Plod on, and each one as before will chase
His favourite phantom; yet all these shall leave
Their mirth and their employments, and shall come,
And make their bed with thee. As the long train
Of ages glides away, the sons of men,
The youth in life's green spring, and he who goes
In the full strength of years, matron, and maid,
And the sweet babe, and the gray-headed man,—
Shall one by one be gathered to thy side,
By those who in their turn shall follow them.

So live, that when thy summons comes to join
The innumerable caravan, which moves
To that mysterious realm, where each shall take
His chamber in the silent halls of death,
Thou go not, like the quarry-slave at night,
Scourged to his dungeon; but, sustained and soothed
By an unfaltering trust, approach thy grave,
Like one who wraps the drapery of his couch
About him, and lies down to pleasant dreams.

Source: William Cullen Bryant, *Poems* (New York: Harper & Brothers, 1836).

Cooper, James Fenimore

(1789–1851)

James Fenimore Cooper was the first novelist to make a living examining distinctly American characters, subjects, and themes. Over the course of his prolific career, in which he produced more than 30 novels as well as short-story collections, travel accounts, histories, and other works, Cooper played a pioneering role in the development of a uniquely American literature while achieving international stature.

Early Years

He was born to William Cooper and Elizabeth Fenimore Cooper on September 15, 1789, in Burlington, New Jersey. William was a successful shopkeeper, politician, and land speculator who bought several thousand acres around Otsego Lake in upstate New York and founded Cooperstown, New York, on its southern shore in 1790. The family moved there when the boy was a year old, allowing his father to become a judge and two-term U.S. congressman while developing the area.

Growing up in Otsego Hall, the family estate completed in 1799, afforded young Cooper the opportunity to explore the surrounding forests, cultivate a love of nature, and experience life in a frontier village firsthand. In this setting, he interacted with Iroquois Indians, white settlers, hunters and trappers, and others who served as models for many of his later characters.

Cooper's formal education began in the village school in Cooperstown, continued under the tutelage of an English rector in Albany, and came to an inauspicious end when Yale College expelled him for pranks after two years, at age 15. According to Cooper, his preparatory studies had made college too easy, leaving him with an excess of free time with which to explore the outdoors, spend his father's money, and get into trouble. After leaving Yale, Cooper studied briefly under a minister in Cooperstown and then found work as a sailor. Although Cooper's family initially opposed a naval career, his father eventually assisted him in finding a place on the merchant ship *Stirling*, which sailed for England in 1806. He was 17.

Upon returning from this trip, Cooper entered the fledgling U.S. Navy, serving on warships at a frontier outpost on Lake Ontario and then recruiting sailors in New York City. He eventually achieved the rank of midshipman. It was also during this period that Cooper met Susan Augusta de Lancey, the daughter of a prominent New York family that had lost much of its wealth during the American Revolution because of its Loyalist sympathies. After leaving the navy, Cooper was married on January 1, 1811. During the course of their marriage, the couple would have seven children—five daughters and two sons.

The Coopers began their married life on the De Lancey property in Westchester County, New York, before moving to a farmhouse near Cooperstown. During this time, Cooper battled serious financial problems. His father had died in 1809 and left an estate that, while large, was deeply indebted. Matters were complicated by the economic havoc wrought by the War of 1812 and the poor management of William Cooper's estate by his sons. James Cooper escaped some of his financial concerns by moving back to the De Lancey property, but he made matters worse by investing in an unprofitable whaling ship and losing even more of his personal property. Ultimately, much of William Cooper's estate had to be sold at auction, leaving James in precarious financial straits and desperately in need of steady income.

Literary Success

According to an account by his daughter Susan, Cooper began writing on a whim. One day, after reading aloud to his family from a poorly written English novel, he declared that he could write a better one. His wife laughed, but Cooper began writing almost immediately. His efforts resulted in *Precaution* (1820), an anonymously published novel of domestic English life. The book

In his Leatherstocking Tales—four novels including *The Last of the Mohicans*—James Fenimore Cooper gave life to the frontier in a new and uniquely American literary style.

met with meager commercial success, but the experience prompted Cooper to continue writing.

His next book was *The Spy* (1821), a romance of the American Revolution set in Westchester County. This one brought Cooper the fame and fortune he wished for, allowing him to give up farming and devote himself to writing full-time. *The Spy* also marked the beginning of Cooper's focus on American topics and themes. He continued on this track with *The Pioneers* (1823), set in a location similar to Cooperstown, with characters who closely resembled his father and older sister. *The Pioneers* was the first in a series of frontier adventures, known as the Leatherstocking Tales, featuring the frontiersman and adventurer Natty Bumppo as protagonist. The series eventually grew to include four more novels: *The Last of the Mohicans* (1826), *The Prairie* (1827), *The Pathfinder* (1840), and *The Deerslayer* (1841). In the meantime, Cooper also produced *The Pilot* (1824), which has been called the first sea novel in the English language.

As Cooper's literary career flourished, he made several major changes in his life. In 1822, he moved the family to New York City, which proved beneficial by putting him in closer touch with his publishers and fellow writers. In 1826, shortly after the publication of *The Last of the Mohicans* and at the height of his popularity, Cooper legally added "Fenimore" to his name in honor of his mother. He also decided to take his family on a trip to Europe. Originally planned for five years, the sojourn was extended to seven. In addition to living in England, France, and Italy, the family traveled throughout the continent. By this time, Cooper's writing had attracted as much attention abroad as it had in America. Thus, while in Europe, he enjoyed the society of Sir Walter Scott and the Marquis de Lafayette, among other notables.

Later Challenges

After 1830, influenced by his experiences in Europe, Cooper expanded his writing to books on travel, democracy, politics, and naval history. He continued to write novels, including a fictional travel series set in America and romances with European settings. Many of these works failed to win the acclaim of either critics or the general public, however, and the trend held for many of Cooper's writings over the remainder of his career.

Upon returning to the United States in 1833, Cooper was unhappy with much of what he found. In particular, his writings of the time reflect his concerns over a political climate that he believed threatened democracy. And his criticisms drew attention. The first of his several works critical of American culture, *A Letter to His Countrymen* (1834), stirred considerable controversy in the press. Cooper did not respond well to the condemnation, airing his grievances in the press and occasionally in court. He pursued libel suits against individuals whom he felt disparaged him unfairly, winning several of them. With his popularity already waning, however, the sale of his books suffered further because of declining public interest in adventure novels.

Cooper also encountered troubles in his personal life. In 1834, he began rebuilding the family estate of Otsego Hall, where he returned with his family and remained settled for the rest of his life. Shortly after arriving, however, he set himself at odds with neighbors over a popular recreational area that he claimed as part of the Cooper estate. His attempts to regain control of the land met with public outrage, including a resolution that declared him "odious to a greater portion of the citizens of this community."

Despite declining popularity and sales, sometimes harsh criticism, and such personal distractions, Cooper continued to write until his death. Of his later works, *The Pathfinder* (1840) and *The Deerslayer* (1841) were the best received. A softening of critical notices and of public opinion in general helped restore some of Cooper's lost stature in his final years. He died of dropsy at Otsego Hall on September 14, 1851.

Literary Legacy

Cooper's literary career was pathbreaking in many respects. He was the first American novelist—and the only one in the first half of the nineteenth century—to earn enough from his writing to support a family. To many in the United States and abroad, his works brought notice to the American literary scene and gave it credibility. His popularity spawned dramatic presentations and art exhibits based on the setting, stories, and characters of his novels, not to mention a slew of literary imitators. He was a cultural superstar of the early nineteenth century whose fictional accounts of America's frontier origins found a mass audience and demonstrated that the public at large could support a distinctive, homegrown American literature.

Certainly, Cooper's work has faced harsh criticism, both during his lifetime and long after his death. Mark Twain, for example, chronicled his defects as a writer in an 1895 essay titled "Fenimore Cooper's Literary Offenses." Nevertheless, several of Cooper's novels remain true classics of American literature; the characters he portrayed—such as the hearty frontiersman and the noble Native American—became part of the national mythology; and his depictions of life in the colonial wilderness have remained indelibly fixed in the American consciousness.

Amy Ann Cox

See also: Environment and Nature, Views of

◇◇

Chapter One, *The Last of the Mohicans,* 1826

◇◇

The second book of his Leatherstocking Tales series, James Fenimore Cooper's historical novel The Last of the Mohicans *is his most widely read work. The story is set in British North America in 1757, the third year of the French and Indian War (or Seven Years' War). Although historic events are often embellished, the novel gave readers a realistic glimpse of colonial frontier life and the relationship between Europeans and Native Americans.*

In Chapter One, reproduced here, Cooper sets the scene—the war between the British and the French—and depicts the forbidding terrain of upstate New York. The French, who have allied with Indian tribes in the region, are moving an army south toward British-held Fort William Henry. The two daughters of the colonel who commands the fort insist on visiting him, traveling with a column of reinforcements. As in Cooper's other best works, the most appealing attributes of The Last of the Mohicans *are its panoramic depictions of the land, vivid imagery, and episodic drama.*

It was a feature peculiar to the colonial wars of North America, that the toils and dangers of the wilderness were to be encountered before the adverse hosts could meet. A wide and apparently an impervious boundary of forests severed the possessions of the hostile provinces of France and England. The hardy colonist, and the trained European who fought at his side, frequently expended months in struggling against the rapids of the streams, or in effecting the rugged passes of the mountains, in quest of an opportunity to exhibit their courage in a more martial conflict. But, emulating the patience and self-denial of the practiced native warriors, they learned to overcome every difficulty; and it would seem that, in time, there was no recess of the woods so dark, nor any secret place so lovely, that it might claim exemption from the inroads of those who had pledged their blood to satiate their vengeance, or to uphold the cold and selfish policy of the distant monarchs of Europe.

Perhaps no district throughout the wide extent of the intermediate frontiers can furnish a livelier picture of the cruelty and fierceness of the savage warfare of those periods than the country which lies between the head waters of the Hudson and the adjacent lakes.

The facilities which nature had there offered to the march of the combatants were too obvious to be neglected. The lengthened sheet of the Champlain stretched from the frontiers of Canada, deep within the borders of the neighboring province of New York, forming a natural passage across half the distance that the French were compelled to master in order to strike their enemies. Near its southern termination, it received the contributions of another lake, whose waters were so limpid as to have been exclusively selected by the Jesuit missionaries to perform the typical purification of baptism, and to obtain for it the title of lake "du Saint Sacrement." The less zealous English thought they conferred a sufficient honor on its unsullied fountains, when they bestowed the name of their reigning prince, the second of the house of Hanover. The two united to rob the untutored possessors of its wooded scenery of their native right to perpetuate its original appellation of "Horican."

Winding its way among countless islands, and imbedded in mountains, the "holy lake" extended a dozen leagues still further to the south. With the high plain that there interposed itself to the further passage of the water, commenced a portage of as many miles, which conducted the adventurer to the banks of the Hudson, at a point where, with the usual obstructions of the rapids, or rifts, as they were then termed in the language of the country, the river became navigable to the tide.

While, in the pursuit of their daring plans of annoyance, the restless enterprise of the French even attempted the distant and difficult gorges of the Alleghany, it may easily be imagined that their proverbial acuteness would not overlook the natural advantages of the district we have just described. It became, emphatically, the bloody arena, in which most of the battles for the mastery of the colonies were contested. Forts were erected at the different points that commanded the facilities of the route, and were taken and retaken, razed and rebuilt, as victory alighted on the hostile banners. While the husbandman shrank back from the dangerous passes, within the safer boundaries of the more ancient settlements, armies larger than those that had often disposed of the scepters of the mother countries, were seen to bury themselves in these forests, whence they rarely returned but in skeleton bands, that were haggard with care or dejected by defeat. Though the arts of peace were unknown to this fatal region, its forests were alive with men; its shades and glens rang with the sounds of martial music, and the echoes of its mountains threw back the laugh, or repeated the wanton cry, of many a gallant and reckless youth, as he hurried by them, in the noontide of his spirits, to slumber in a long night of forgetfulness.

It was in this scene of strife and bloodshed that the incidents we shall attempt to relate occurred, during the third year of the war which England and France last waged for the possession of a country that neither was destined to retain.

The imbecility of her military leaders abroad, and the fatal want of energy in her councils at home, had lowered the character of Great Britain from the proud elevation on which it had been placed by the talents and enterprise of her former warriors and statesmen. No longer dreaded by her enemies, her servants were fast losing the confidence of self-respect. In this mortifying abasement, the colonists, though innocent of her imbecility, and too humble to be the agents of her blunders, were but the natural participators. They had recently seen a chosen army from that country, which, reverencing as a mother, they had blindly believed invincible—an army led by a chief who had been selected from a crowd of trained warriors, for his rare military endowments, disgracefully routed by a handful of French and Indians, and only saved from annihilation by the coolness and spirit of a Virginian boy, whose riper fame has since diffused itself, with the steady influence of moral truth, to the uttermost confines of Christendom. A wide frontier had been laid naked by this unexpected disaster, and more substantial evils were preceded by a thousand fanciful and imaginary dangers. The alarmed colonists believed that the yells of the savages mingled with every fitful gust of wind that issued from the interminable forests of the west. The terrific character of their merciless enemies increased immeasurably the natural horrors of warfare. Numberless recent massacres were still vivid in their recollections; nor was there any ear in the provinces so deaf as not to have drunk in with avidity the narrative of some fearful tale of midnight murder, in which the natives of the forests were the principal and barbarous actors. As the credulous and excited traveler related the hazardous chances of the wilderness, the blood of the timid curdled with terror, and mothers cast anxious glances even at those children which slumbered within the security of the largest towns. In short, the magnifying influence of fear began to set at naught the calculations of reason, and to render those who should have remembered their manhood, the slaves of the basest passions. Even the most confident and the stoutest hearts began to think the issue of the contest was becoming doubtful; and that abject class was hourly increasing in numbers, who thought they foresaw all the possessions of the English crown in America subdued by their Christian foes, or laid waste by the inroads of their relentless allies.

The alarmed colonists believed that the yells of the savages mingled with every fitful gust of wind that issued from the interminable forests of the west.

When, therefore, intelligence was received at the fort which covered the southern termination of the portage between the Hudson and the lakes, that Montcalm had been seen moving up the Champlain, with an army "numerous as the leaves on the trees," its truth was admitted with more of the craven reluctance of fear than with the stern joy that a warrior should feel, in finding an enemy within reach of his blow. The news had been brought, toward the decline of a day in midsummer, by an Indian runner, who also bore an urgent request from Munro, the commander of a work on the shore of the "holy lake," for a speedy and powerful reinforcement. It has already been mentioned that the distance between these two posts was less than five leagues. The rude path, which originally formed their line of communication, had been widened for the passage of wagons; so that the distance which had been traveled by the son of the forest in two hours, might easily be effected by a detachment of troops, with their necessary baggage, between the rising and setting of a summer sun. The loyal servants of the British crown had given to one of these forest-fastnesses the name of William Henry, and to the other that of Fort Edward, calling each after a favorite prince of the reigning family. The veteran Scotchman just named held the first, with a regiment of regulars and a few provincials; a force really by far too small to make head against the formidable power that Montcalm was leading to the foot of his earthen mounds. At the latter, however, lay General Webb, who commanded the armies of the king in the northern provinces, with a body of more than five thousand men. By uniting the several detachments of his command, this officer might have arrayed nearly double that number of combatants against the enterprising Frenchman, who had ventured so far from his reinforcements, with an army but little superior in numbers.

But under the influence of their degraded fortunes, both officers and men appeared better disposed to await the approach of their formidable antagonists, within their works, than to resist the progress of their march, by emulating the successful example of the French at Fort du Quesne, and striking a blow on their advance.

After the first surprise of the intelligence had a little abated, a rumor was spread through the entrenched camp, which stretched along the margin of the Hudson, forming a chain of outworks to the body of the fort itself, that a chosen detachment of fifteen hundred men was to depart, with the dawn, for William Henry, the post at the northern extremity of the portage. That which at first was only rumor, soon became certainty, as orders passed from the quarters of the commander-in-chief to the several corps he had selected for this service, to prepare for their speedy departure. All doubts as to the intention of Webb now vanished, and an hour or two of hurried footsteps and anxious faces succeeded. The novice in the military art flew from point to point, retarding his own preparations by the excess of his violent and somewhat distempered zeal; while the more practiced veteran made his arrangements with a deliberation that scorned every appearance of haste; though his sober lineaments and anxious eye sufficiently betrayed that he had no very strong professional relish for the, as yet, untried and dreaded warfare of the wilderness. At length the sun set in a flood of glory, behind the distant western hills, and as darkness drew its veil around the secluded spot the sounds of preparation diminished; the last light finally disappeared from the log cabin of some officer; the trees cast their deeper shadows over the mounds and the rippling stream, and a silence soon pervaded the camp, as deep as that which reigned in the vast forest by which it was environed.

According to the orders of the preceding night, the heavy sleep of the army was broken by the rolling of the warning drums, whose rattling echoes were heard issuing, on the damp morning air, out of every vista of the woods, just as day began to draw the shaggy outlines of some tall pines of the vicinity, on the opening brightness of a soft and cloudless eastern sky. In an instant the whole camp was in motion; the meanest soldier arousing from his lair to witness the departure of his comrades, and to share in the excitement and incidents of the hour. The simple array of the chosen band was soon completed. While the regular and trained hirelings of the king marched with haughtiness to the right of the line, the less pretending colonists took their humbler position on its left, with a docility that long practice had rendered easy. The scouts departed; strong guards preceded and followed the lumbering vehicles that bore the baggage; and before the gray light of the morning was mellowed by the rays of the sun, the main body of the combatants wheeled into column, and left the encampment with a show of high military bearing, that served to drown the slumbering apprehensions of many a novice, who was now about to make his first essay in arms. While in view of their admiring comrades, the same proud front and ordered array was observed, until the notes of their fifes growing fainter in distance, the forest at length appeared to swallow up the living mass which had slowly entered its bosom.

The deepest sounds of the retiring and invisible column had ceased to be borne on the breeze to the listeners, and the latest straggler had already disappeared in pursuit; but there still remained the signs of another departure, before a log cabin of unusual size and accommodations, in front of which those sentinels paced their rounds, who were known to guard the person of the English general. At this spot were gathered some half dozen horses, caparisoned in a manner which showed that two, at least, were destined to bear the persons of females, of a rank that it was not usual to meet so far in the wilds of the country. A third wore trappings and arms of an officer of the staff; while the rest, from the plainness of the housings, and the traveling mails with which they were encumbered, were evidently fitted for the reception of as many menials, who were, seemingly, already waiting the pleasure of those they served. At a respectful distance from this unusual show, were gathered divers groups of curious idlers; some admiring the blood and bone of the high-mettled military charger, and others gazing at the preparations, with the dull wonder of vulgar curiosity. There was one man, however, who, by his countenance and actions, formed a marked exception to those who composed the latter class of spectators, being neither idle, nor seemingly very ignorant.

The person of this individual was to the last degree ungainly, without being in any particular manner deformed. He had all the bones and joints of other men, without any of their proportions. Erect, his stature surpassed that of his fellows; though seated, he appeared reduced within the ordinary limits of the race. The same contrariety in his members seemed to exist throughout the whole man. His head was large; his shoulders narrow; his arms long and dangling; while his hands were small, if not delicate. His legs and thighs were thin, nearly to emaciation, but of extraordinary length; and his knees would have been considered tremendous, had they not been outdone by the broader foundations on which this false superstructure of blended human orders was so profanely reared. The ill-assorted and injudicious attire of the individual only served to render his awkwardness more conspicuous. A sky-blue coat, with short and broad skirts and low cape, exposed a long, thin neck, and longer and thinner legs, to the worst animadversions of the evil-disposed. His nether garment was a yellow nankeen, closely fitted to the shape, and tied at his bunches of knees by large knots of white ribbon, a good deal sullied by use. Clouded cotton stockings, and shoes, on one of the latter of which was a plated spur, completed the costume of the lower extremity of this figure, no curve or angle of which was concealed, but, on the other hand, studiously exhibited, through the vanity or simplicity of its owner.

From beneath the flap of an enormous pocket of a soiled vest of embossed silk, heavily ornamented with tarnished silver lace, projected an instrument, which, from being seen in such martial company, might have been easily mistaken for some mischievous and unknown implement of war. Small as it was, this uncommon engine had excited the curiosity of most of the Europeans in the camp, though several of the provincials were seen to handle it, not only without fear, but with the utmost familiarity. A large, civil cocked hat, like those worn by clergymen within the last thirty years, surmounted the whole, furnishing dignity to a good-natured and somewhat vacant countenance, that apparently needed such artificial aid, to support the gravity of some high and extraordinary trust.

While the common herd stood aloof, in deference to the quarters of Webb, the figure we have described stalked into the center of the domestics, freely expressing his censures or commendations on the merits of the horses, as by chance they displeased or satisfied his judgment.

"This beast, I rather conclude, friend, is not of home raising, but is from foreign lands, or perhaps from the little island itself over the blue water?" he said, in a voice as remarkable for the softness and sweetness of its tones, as was his person for its rare proportions; "I may speak of these things, and be no braggart; for I have been down at both havens; that which is situate at the mouth of Thames, and is named after the capital of Old England, and that which is called 'Haven,' with the addition of the word 'New'; and have seen the scows and brigantines collecting their droves, like the gathering to the ark, being outward bound to the Island of Jamaica, for the purpose of barter and traffic in four-footed animals; but never before have I beheld a beast which verified the true scripture war-horse like this: 'He paweth in the valley, and rejoiceth in his strength; he goeth on to meet the armed men. He saith among the trumpets, Ha, ha; and he smelleth the battle afar off, the thunder of the captains, and the shouting.' It would seem that the stock of the horse of Israel had descended to our own time; would it not, friend?"

Receiving no reply to this extraordinary appeal, which in truth, as it was delivered with the vigor of full and sonorous tones, merited some sort of notice, he who had thus sung forth the language of the holy book turned to the silent figure to whom he had unwittingly addressed himself, and found a new and more powerful subject of admiration in the object that encountered his gaze. His eyes fell on the still, upright, and rigid form of the "Indian runner," who had borne to the camp the unwelcome tidings of the preceding evening. Although in a state of perfect repose, and apparently disregarding, with characteristic stoicism, the excitement and bustle around him, there was a sullen fierceness mingled with the quiet of the savage, that was likely to arrest the attention of much more experienced eyes than those which now scanned him, in unconcealed amazement. The native bore both the tomahawk and knife of his tribe; and yet his appearance was not altogether that of a warrior. On the contrary, there was an air of neglect about his person, like that which might have proceeded from great and recent exertion, which he had not yet found leisure to repair. The colors of the war-paint had blended in dark confusion about his fierce countenance, and rendered his swarthy lineaments still more savage and repulsive than if art had attempted an effect which had been thus produced by chance. His eye, alone, which glistened like a fiery star amid lowering clouds, was to be seen in its state of native wildness. For a single instant his searching and yet wary glance met the wondering look of the other, and then changing its direction, partly in cunning, and partly in disdain, it remained fixed, as if penetrating the distant air.

It is impossible to say what unlooked-for remark this short and silent communication, between two such singular men, might have elicited from the white man, had not his active curiosity been again drawn to other objects. A general movement among the domestics, and a low sound of gentle voices, announced the approach of those whose presence alone was wanted to enable the cavalcade to move. The simple admirer of the war-horse instantly fell back to a low, gaunt, switch-tailed mare, that was unconsciously gleaning the faded herbage of the camp nigh by; where, leaning with one elbow on the blanket that concealed an apology for a saddle, he became a spectator of the departure, while a foal was quietly making its morning repast, on the opposite side of the same animal.

A young man, in the dress of an officer, conducted to their steeds two females, who, as it was apparent by their dresses, were prepared to encounter the fatigues of a journey in the woods. One, and she was the more juvenile in her appearance, though both were young, permitted glimpses of her dazzling complexion, fair golden hair, and bright blue eyes, to be caught, as she artlessly suffered the morning air to blow aside the green veil which descended low from her beaver.

The flush which still lingered above the pines in the western sky was not more bright nor delicate than the bloom on her cheek; nor was the opening day more cheering than the animated smile which she bestowed on the youth, as he assisted her into the saddle. The other, who appeared to share equally in the attention of the young officer, concealed her charms from the gaze of the soldiery with a care that seemed better fitted to the experience of four or five additional years. It could be seen, however, that her person, though molded with the same exquisite proportions, of which none of the graces were lost by the traveling dress she wore, was rather fuller and more mature than that of her companion.

No sooner were these females seated, than their attendant sprang lightly into the saddle of the war-horse, when the whole three bowed to Webb, who in courtesy, awaited their parting on the threshold of his cabin and turning their horses' heads, they proceeded at a slow amble, followed by their train, toward the northern entrance of the encampment. As they traversed that short distance, not a voice was heard among them; but a slight exclamation proceeded from the younger of the females, as the

Indian runner glided by her, unexpectedly, and led the way along the military road in her front. Though this sudden and startling movement of the Indian produced no sound from the other, in the surprise her veil also was allowed to open its folds, and betrayed an indescribable look of pity, admiration, and horror, as her dark eye followed the easy motions of the savage. The tresses of this lady were shining and black, like the plumage of the raven. Her complexion was not brown, but it rather appeared charged with the color of the rich blood, that seemed ready to burst its bounds. And yet there was neither coarseness nor want of shadowing in a countenance that was exquisitely regular, and dignified and surpassingly beautiful. She smiled, as if in pity at her own momentary forgetfulness, discovering by the act a row of teeth that would have shamed the purest ivory; when, replacing the veil, she bowed her face, and rode in silence, like one whose thoughts were abstracted from the scene around her.

Sources: Open Library (http://openlibrary.org); J. Fenimore Cooper, *The Last of the Mohicans* (New York: John W. Lovell, 1800).

Emerson, Ralph Waldo

(1803–1882)

Perhaps no individual contributed more to American letters in the nineteenth century than Ralph Waldo Emerson. His writings and thought—a fusion of literature, philosophy, religion, and politics—influenced a generation of American authors, from Henry David Thoreau and Frederick Douglass to Margaret Fuller and Louisa May Alcott. Emerson is remembered today as the leader of the Transcendentalist movement.

Little in Emerson's early life hinted at the prominence that lay ahead. Born in Boston on May 25, 1803, he was the second of five surviving boys in a family as old as the first New England settlement. When his father, a Unitarian pastor, died in 1811, the Emersons were left with little financial security or promise. Emerson's mother was forced to transform the family home into a boardinghouse, and with the help of her sister-in-law, she labored to provide her sons with satisfactory educations.

Emerson attended the Boston Latin School, where he wrote his first poems, and then enrolled at Harvard at the age of 14. Graduating thirtieth in a class of 59, he began keeping a list of the books he had read and a journal that would remain a lifelong endeavor. "I do hereby nominate & appoint 'Imagination,'" Emerson began, "the generalissimo & chief marshall of all the luckless ragamuffin Ideas." What he called his "Wide World" or "Savings Bank"—the jottings and observations in these journals, which eventually totaled 182 in all—served as the basis for the lectures and essays he would write later in his career.

After a few years of teaching in and around Boston, Emerson enrolled in Harvard's Divinity School in 1825, though he never took a degree from the institution. In March 1829, he was ordained as the junior pastor of Boston's Second Church, following nine generations of Emersons into the ministry. Four months later, Emerson married Ellen Louisa Tucker, age 17, already ill with tuberculosis. Ellen would die in less than two years' time, leaving Emerson distraught. As he lamented to his Aunt Mary, "My angel is gone to heaven this morning & I am alone in the world."

Change in Direction

Turmoil and instability persisted for Emerson, who in 1832 made the decision to resign his ministry. Although he belonged to a liberal denomination—the Unitarians—he chafed under the constraints of any creed. Emerson confessed in his journal, "My business is with the living. . . . I have sometimes thought that in order to be a good minister it was necessary to leave the ministry." Rejecting institutional restrictions and practices, such as the administration of the Eucharist, Emerson believed in the power of inner faith and the guidance of self-determination, central themes of the essays he would later write. In Emerson's worldview, no church was necessary to experience a connection to God: The soul links all to the divine.

A small inheritance from his wife's death enabled Emerson to set sail for Europe on Christmas Day 1832. While on tour, he met a number of the literary titans he had admired from across the ocean: Thomas Carlyle, Samuel Taylor Coleridge, William Wordsworth, and others. In 1833, Emerson returned to the United States rejuvenated, eager to write and to determine "where & how to live." He settled in rural Concord, Massachusetts, and began participating in the developing lyceum movement—lectures serving as an easy transition away from the pulpit and providing a modest salary. In the years to come, Emerson would marry Lydia Jackson (in 1835), father four children, and form two crucial life friendships—with Henry David Thoreau and with the journalist and women's rights advocate Margaret Fuller. Emerson would later lend Thoreau property at Walden Pond for the latter's famed experiment in independent living, while Fuller helped Emerson found and edit *The Dial,* a short-lived but well-read New England periodical.

More than any other activity, lecturing solidified Emerson's reputation as an intellectual. Between the mid-1830s and the close of his career more than 40 years later, he delivered some 1,500 public lectures. His orations covered diverse topics, including such hot-button subjects as temperance, women's rights, and personal ethics. As his acclaim grew, Emerson traveled from the lyceum circuit of New England to the lecture halls of New York, the Middle Atlantic states, and, late in life, California.

Transcendentalism

In 1836, Emerson anonymously published his first book, the essay *Nature*, though its authorship was quickly recognized. One of the first lines declared his purpose: "All science has one aim, namely, to find a theory of nature." In short, Emerson offered in *Nature* a prescription for living in the universe, encouraging readers to find in the natural world answers to eternal questions of being. The ideas in *Nature* served as a foundation for the Transcendentalist movement— a philosophy that emphasizes the connectedness of all beings, the innate goodness of humankind, the importance of intuition and imagination, and the need for social and religious reform.

Emerson followed the publication of *Nature* with several lectures and addresses. Most notable among these were the 1837 "American Scholar" lecture to the Harvard Phi Beta Kappa society and the 1838 Divinity School "Address." The former was described as America's "Intellectual Declaration of Independence," articulating the proper role of the scholar in a democratic society. According to Emerson, adherence to the traditions of European writing had thwarted the development of American national art: "Meek young men grow up in libraries, believing it their duty to accept the views, which Cicero, which Locke, which Bacon, have given, forgetful that Cicero, Locke, and Bacon were only young men in libraries, when they wrote those books."

Whereas the "American Scholar" lecture encouraged young writers to reject outmoded literary conventions, the "Address" at Harvard's Divinity School critiqued the religious establishment of the day. Emerson feared that the power of faith was being threatened by a spiritually deadened reading of the Bible. He longed to "acquaint men at first hand with the Deity" and urged his listeners to end their deference to the clergy: "I look for the hour when that Supreme Beauty, which ravished the souls of Eastern men, and chiefly of those Hebrews, and through their lips spoke oracles to all time, shall speak in the West also." The incendiary speech earned Emerson

As leader of the Transcendentalist movement, essayist and poet Ralph Waldo Emerson championed American cultural independence and the innate power of the free human spirit.

a 30-year ban from speaking at the university but made him a widely sought-after spokesman for radical, reformist positions.

Emerson's more abstract ideas about scholarship, religion, and personal autonomy were always grounded in firm convictions about political justice and social action. In a letter to President Martin Van Buren in 1838, he decried the removal of the Cherokee Nation from its homeland east of the Mississippi River. Throughout his career, Emerson was similarly vocal in his support for the abolitionist movement. After passage of the Fugitive Slave Law in 1850, he delivered an impassioned protest in which he declared, "An immoral law makes it a man's duty to break it, at every hazard. . . . If our resistance to this law is not right, there is no right."

Essayist

Emerson published his most renowned essays in the 1840s. The most famous, "Self-Reliance," appeared in the collection *Essays* (1841). In it, he underscores the values of self-confidence and integrity. "Whoso would be a man," he wrote, "must be a nonconformist." In many of his essays of the 1840s, however, Emerson balanced his emphasis on strong, willful individualism with a belief in the interconnectedness of all living things. "Within the form of every creature," he declared in "The Poet," "is a force impelling it to ascend into a higher form." The stress on ascension and metamorphosis bears the hallmarks of Emerson's Transcendentalist worldview—attachment to change and revolution coupled with faith in the unity of existence.

Emerson's affirmative view of life was challenged in 1842, when his beloved son Waldo died of scarlet fever. The writings that came out of this tragedy—namely, the essay "Experience" and the elegy "Threnody"—bear witness to the extent of Emerson's spiritual crisis. In 1844, he published another volume, *Essays: Second Series,* which blends his signature style with the melancholy realities of his recent loss. In 1846, Emerson published his first book of poetry, titled simply *Poems.* The slender volume received positive reviews from critics, many of whom found his tetrameter lines innovative and visionary.

Despite his distaste for discipleship, Emerson's fame brought him a legion of acolytes. On a lecture tour of the Northeast, for example, his daughter recalled "seeing all the world burn incense to Father." By the time of the Civil War, Emerson had become something of a national treasure. At the 1863 International Exposition in Paris, his portrait hung beside such other American icons as Albert Bierstadt's painting of the Rocky Mountains and Frederic Edwin Church's depiction of Niagara Falls. Emerson had become the face of American letters.

Deeply troubled by the outbreak of the Civil War, Emerson eventually came to view the conflict as an opportunity for national cleansing. He used his fame to draw attention to the cause of emancipation, delivering several prominent addresses on the issue. He was profoundly gratified by the Emancipation Proclamation and equally saddened by the assassination of President Lincoln.

In the years after the war, Emerson continued to publish and lecture, though his productivity never again reached the heights of the 1840s. His tone remained hopeful and his goals grandiose, an exuberant nationalism always at the core of his writings. Walt Whitman famously remarked, "I was simmering, simmering, simmering, and Emerson brought me to a boil."

Ralph Waldo Emerson died of pneumonia on April 27, 1882. His desire to undermine all forms of authority, whether religious, political, or literary, remained the recurring theme of his writings to the end. As Emerson put it, "I unsettle all things. No facts are to me sacred; none are profane; I simply experiment, an endless seeker, with no past at my back."

Nicholas Soodik

See also: Environment and Nature, Views of; Fuller, Margaret; Libraries and Lyceums; Poetry; Thoreau, Henry David; Transcendentalism

"The American Scholar" (excerpts), 1851

In his address to Harvard's Phi Beta Kappa Society on August 31, 1837, titled "The American Scholar," Ralph Waldo Emerson called on the American intellectual and literary community to free itself from the traditions and prejudices of the European past—no matter its achievements—and to forge a unique culture based on immediate experience of the New World. In what Oliver Wendell Holmes hailed as America's "Intellectual Declaration of Independence," Emerson envisioned a higher wisdom—one rooted in nature, informed by action, and driven by unfettered individual minds.

Mr. President and Gentlemen,

I greet you on the re-commencement of our literary year. Our anniversary is one of hope, and, perhaps, not enough of labor. We do not meet for games of strength or skill, for the recitation of histories, tragedies, and odes, like the ancient Greeks; for parliaments of love and poesy, like the Troubadours; nor for the advancement of science, like our cotemporaries in the British and European capitals. Thus far, our holiday has been simply a friendly sign of the survival of the love of letters amongst a people too busy to give to letters any more. As such, it is precious as the sign of an indestructible instinct. Perhaps the time is already come, when it ought to be, and will be, something else; when the sluggard intellect of this continent will look from under its iron lids, and fill the postponed expectation of the world with something better than the exertions of mechanical skill. Our day of dependence, our long apprenticeship to the learning of other lands, draws to a close. The millions, that around us are rushing into life, cannot always be fed on the sere remains of foreign harvests. Events, actions arise, that must be sung, that will sing themselves. Who can doubt, that poetry will revive and lead in a new age, as the star in the constellation Harp, which now flames in our zenith, astronomers announce, shall one day be the pole-star for a thousand years?

In this hope, I accept the topic which not only usage, but the nature of our association, seem to prescribe to this day,—the AMERICAN SCHOLAR. Year by year, we come up hither to read one more chapter of his biography. Let us inquire what light new days and events have thrown on his character, and his hopes. . . .

I. The first in time and the first in importance of the influences upon the mind is that of nature. Every day, the sun; and, after sunset, night and her stars. Ever the winds blow; ever the grass grows. Every day, men and women, conversing, beholding and beholden. The scholar is he of all men whom this spectacle most engages. He must settle its value in his mind. What is nature to him? There is never a beginning, there is never an end, to the inexplicable continuity of this web of God, but always circular power returning into itself. Therein it resembles his own spirit, whose beginning, whose ending, he never can find,—so entire, so boundless. Far, too, as her splendors shine, system on system shooting like rays, upward, downward, without centre, without circumference,—in the mass and in the particle, nature hastens to render account of herself to the mind. Classification begins. To the young mind, every thing is individual, stands by itself. By and by, it finds how to join two things, and see in them one nature; then three, then three thousand; and so, tyrannized over

Perhaps the time is already come . . .
when the sluggard intellect of this
continent will look from under its iron lids.

by its own unifying instinct, it goes on tying things together, diminishing anomalies, discovering roots running under ground, whereby contrary and remote things cohere, and flower out from one stem. It presently learns, that, since the dawn of history, there has been a constant accumulation and classifying of facts. But what is classification but the perceiving that these objects are not chaotic, and are not foreign, but have a law which is also a law of the human mind? The astronomer discovers that geometry, a pure abstraction of the human mind, is the measure of planetary motion. The chemist finds proportions and intelligible method throughout matter; and science is nothing but the finding of analogy, identity, in the most remote parts. The ambitious soul sits down before each refractory fact; one after another, reduces all strange constitutions, all new powers, to their class and their law, and goes on for ever to animate the last fibre of organization, the outskirts of nature, by insight.

Thus to him, to this school-boy under the bending dome of day, is suggested, that he and it proceed from one root; one is leaf and one is flower; relation, sympathy, stirring in every vein. And what is that Root? Is not that the soul of his soul?—A thought too bold,—a dream too wild. Yet when this spiritual light shall have revealed the law of more earthly natures,—when he has learned to worship the soul, and to see that the natural philosophy that now is, is only the first gropings of its gigantic hand, he shall look forward to an ever expanding knowledge as to a becoming creator. He shall see, that nature is the opposite of the soul, answering to it part for part. One is seal, and one is print. Its beauty is the beauty of his own mind. Its laws are the laws of his own mind. Nature then becomes to him the measure of his attainments. So much of nature as he is ignorant of, so much of his own mind does he not yet possess. And, in fine, the ancient precept, "Know thyself," and the modern precept, "Study nature," become at last one maxim.

II. The next great influence into the spirit of the scholar, is, the mind of the Past,—in whatever form, whether of literature, of art, of institutions, that mind is inscribed. Books are the best type of the influence of the past, and perhaps we shall get at the truth,—learn the amount of this influence more conveniently,—by considering their value alone.

The theory of books is noble. The scholar of the first age received into him the world around; brooded thereon; gave it the new arrangement of his own mind, and uttered it again. It came into him, life; it went out from him, truth. It came to him, short-lived actions; it went out from him, immortal thoughts. It came to him, business; it went from him, poetry. It was dead fact; now, it is quick thought. It can stand, and it can go. It now endures, it now flies, it now inspires. Precisely in proportion to the depth of mind from which it issued, so high does it soar, so long does it sing.

Or, I might say, it depends on how far the process had gone, of transmuting life into truth. In proportion to the completeness of the distillation, so will the purity and imperishableness of the product be. But none is quite perfect. As no air-pump can by any means make a perfect vacuum, so neither can any artist entirely exclude the conventional, the local, the perishable from his book, or write a book of pure thought, that shall be as efficient, in all respects, to a remote posterity, as to cotemporaries, or rather to the second age. Each age, it is found, must write its own books; or rather, each generation for the next succeeding. The books of an older period will not fit this.

Yet hence arises a grave mischief. The sacredness which attaches to the act of creation,—the act of thought,—is transferred to the record. The poet chanting, was felt to be a divine man: henceforth the chant is divine also. The writer was a just and wise spirit: henceforward it is settled, the book is perfect; as love of the hero corrupts into worship of his statue. Instantly, the book becomes noxious: the guide is a tyrant. The sluggish and perverted mind of the multitude, slow to open to the incursions of Reason, having once so opened, having once received this book, stands upon it, and makes an outcry, if it is disparaged. Colleges are built on it. Books are written on it by thinkers, not by Man Thinking; by men of talent, that is, who start wrong, who set out from accepted dogmas, not from their own sight of principles. Meek young men grow up in libraries, believing it their duty to accept the views, which Cicero, which Locke, which Bacon, have given, forgetful that Cicero, Locke, and Bacon were only young men in libraries, when they wrote these books.

Hence, instead of Man Thinking, we have the bookworm. Hence, the book-learned class, who value books, as such; not as related to nature and the human constitution, but as making a sort of Third Estate with the world and the soul. Hence, the restorers of readings, the emendators, the bibliomaniacs of all degrees.

Books are the best of things, well used; abused, among the worst. What is the right use? What is the one end, which all means go to effect? They are for nothing but to inspire. I had better never see a book, than to be warped by its attraction clean out of my own orbit, and made a satellite instead of a system. The one thing in the world, of value, is the active soul. This every man is entitled to; this every man contains within him, although, in almost all men, obstructed, and as yet unborn. The soul active sees absolute truth; and utters truth, or creates. In this action, it is genius; not the privilege of here and there a favorite, but the sound estate of every man. In its essence, it is progressive. The book, the college, the school of art, the institution of any kind, stop with some past utterance of genius. This is good, say they,— let us hold by this. They pin me down. They look backward and not forward. But genius looks forward: the eyes of man are set in his forehead, not in his hindhead: man hopes: genius creates. Whatever talents may be, if the man create not, the pure efflux of the Deity is not his;—cinders and smoke there may be, but not yet flame. There are creative manners, there are creative actions, and creative words; manners, actions, words, that is, indicative of no custom or authority, but springing spontaneous from the mind's own sense of good and fair. . . .

Of course, there is a portion of reading quite indispensable to a wise man. History and exact science he must learn by laborious reading. Colleges, in like manner, have their indispensable office,—to teach elements. But they can only highly serve us, when they aim not to drill, but to create; when they gather from far every ray of various genius to their hospitable halls, and, by the concentrated fires, set the hearts of their youth on flame. Thought and knowledge are natures in which apparatus and pretension avail nothing. Gowns, and pecuniary foundations, though of towns of gold, can never countervail the least sentence or syllable of wit. Forget this, and our American colleges will recede in their public importance, whilst they grow richer every year. . . .

Our age is bewailed as the age of Introversion. Must that needs be evil? We, it seems, are critical; we are embarrassed with second thoughts; we cannot enjoy anything for hankering to know whereof the pleasure consists; we are lined with eyes; we see with our feet; the time is infected with Hamlet's unhappiness,—
"Sicklied o'er with the pale cast of thought."
Is it so bad then? Sight is the last thing to be pitied. Would we be blind? Do we fear lest we should outsee nature and God, and drink truth dry? I look upon the discontent of the literary class as a mere announcement of the fact that they find themselves not in the state as untried; as a boy dreads the water before he has learned that he can swim. If there is any period one would desire to be born in, is it not the age of Revolution; when the old and the new stand side by side and admit of being compared; when the energies of all men are searched by fear and by hope; when the historic glories of the old can be compensated by the rich possibilities of the new era? This time, like all times, is a very good one, if we but know what to do with it.

I read with some joy of the auspicious signs of the coming days, as they glimmer already through poetry and art, through philosophy and science, through church and state.

One of these signs is the fact that the same movement which effected the elevation of what was called the lowest class in the state, assumed in literature a very marked and as benign an aspect. Instead of the sublime and beautiful, the near, the low, the common, was explored and poetized. That which had been negligently trodden under foot by those who were harnessing and provisioning themselves for long journeys into far countries, is suddenly found to be richer than all foreign parts. The literature of the poor, the feelings of the child, the philosophy of the street, the meaning of household life, are the topics of the time. It is a great stride. It is a sign, is it not? of new vigor when the extremities are made active, when currents of warm life run into the hands and the feet. I ask not for the great, the remote, the romantic; what is doing in Italy or Arabia; what is Greek art, or Provencal minstrelsy; I embrace the common, I explore and sit at the feet of the familiar, the low. Give me insight into today, and you may have the antique and future worlds. What would

We have listened too long to the courtly muses of Europe.

we really know the meaning of? The meal in the firkin; the milk in the pan; the ballad in the street; the news of the boat; the glance of the eye; the form and the gait of the body;—show me the ultimate reason of these matters; show me the sublime presence of the highest spiritual cause lurking, as always it does lurk, in these suburbs and extremities of nature; let me see every trifle bristling with the polarity that ranges it instantly on an eternal law; and the shop, the plough, and the ledger referred to the like cause by which light undulates and poets sing;—and the world lies no longer a dull miscellany and lumber-room but has form and order; there is no trifle, there is no puzzle, but one design unites and animates the farthest pinnacle and the lowest trench. . . .

The scholar is that man who must take up into himself all the ability of the time, all the contributions of the past, all the hopes of the future. He must be an university of knowledges. If there be one lesson more than another, which should pierce his ear, it is, The world is nothing, the man is all; in yourself is the law of all nature, and you know not yet how a globule of sap ascends; in yourself slumbers the whole of Reason; it is for you to know all, it is for you to dare all.

Mr. President and Gentlemen, this confidence in the unsearched might of man belongs, by all motives, by all prophecy, by all preparation, to the American Scholar. We have listened too long to the courtly muses of Europe. The spirit of the American freeman is already suspected to be timid, imitative, tame. Public and private avarice make the air we breathe thick and fat. The scholar is decent, indolent, complaisant. See already the tragic consequence. The mind of this country, taught to aim at low objects, eats upon itself. There is no work for any but the decorous and the complaisant. Young men of the fairest promise, who begin life upon our shores, inflated by the mountain winds, shined upon by all the stars of God, find the earth below not in unison with these,—but are hindered from action by the disgust which the principles on which business is managed inspire, and turn drudges, or die of disgust,—some of them suicides. What is the remedy? They did not yet see, and thousands of young men as hopeful now crowding to the barriers for the career, do not yet see, that, if the single man plant himself indomitably on his instincts, and there abide, the huge world will come round to him. Patience,—patience;— with the shades of all the good and great for company; and for solace, the perspective of your own infinite life; and for work, the study and the communication of principles, the making those instincts prevalent, the conversion of the world. Is it not the chief disgrace in the world, not to be an unit;—not to be reckoned one character;—not to yield that peculiar fruit which each man was created to bear, but to be reckoned in the gross, in the hundred, or the thousand, of the party, the section, to which we belong; and our opinion predicted geographically, as the north, or the south? Not so, brothers and friends,—please God, ours shall not be so. We will walk on our own feet; we will work with our own hands; we will speak our own minds. The study of letters shall be no longer a name for pity, for doubt, and for sensual indulgence. The dread of man and the love of man shall be a wall of defence and a wreath of joy around all. A nation of men will for the first time exist, because each believes himself inspired by the Divine Soul which also inspires all men.

Source: Ralph Waldo Emerson, *Essays by Ralph Waldo Emerson* (New York: Charles E. Merrill, 1907).

Environment and Nature, Views of

From the end of the Revolutionary War to the start of the Civil War, the United States expanded from a collection of tiny seacoast states to one of the largest continental nations in the world. As conditions changed over the course of those eight decades, attitudes toward the environment changed along with them. Much as it had been for the earlier European settlers, the American landscape in the early days of the republic was an object of awe and wonder, as well as an obstacle to be conquered. As the nation established its cultural independence from Europe, the wonders of the natural environment became a particular source of pride and identity. Western exploration and settlement, the passing of colonial pastoralism, and the first rumblings of the Industrial Revolution brought further changes in attitude. Throughout, the great works and movements in American literature—from early frontier journals and the novels of Cooper, Melville, and Hawthorne to Romantic poetry and the essays of the Transcendentalists—reflected these shifting views of the natural environment.

Early Attitudes

From the time of Christopher Columbus, European explorers and settlers were struck by the newness of the New World, emphasizing the wondrous qualities of the landscape, its flora, and its fauna. The scale, diversity, and beauty of American nature remained marvelous to residents of North America in the succeeding centuries, but the natural landscape was daunting as well.

Puritan leader William Bradford described the country surrounding Plymouth Plantation as "a howling wilderness." For the early English settlers, that wilderness was first and foremost an obstacle to clearing and cultivating farmland. As Bradford and other Puritan writers of the seventeenth century made clear, the wilderness of early America was also a metaphor for metaphysical evil, an attitude that Nathaniel Hawthorne evoked in such antebellum short stories as "Young Goodman Brown" (1835) and "Roger Malvin's Burial" (1835) and the novel *The Scarlet Letter* (1850).

In contrast to these early representations of a forbidding or threatening wilderness, writers of promotional literature in the seventeenth century and field naturalists in the eighteenth century portrayed the American environment as a rich and inviting place. The wide variety of attitudes toward nature in the early republic can be seen in a trio of famous works: Thomas Jefferson's *Notes on the State of Virginia* (1785), William Bartram's *Travels Through North and South Carolina, Georgia, East and West Florida . . .* (1791), and Meriwether Lewis and William Clark's *Journals of Lewis and Clark* (1804–1806).

Jefferson's *Notes* presents a blend of scientific observation, nationalistic argument, and literary description. His description of Virginia's Natural Bridge, for example, emphasizes the precise form and measurements of the geological formation, but it also records an observer's headache upon looking down from the arch of the bridge and the sublime delight of then looking out to the Blue Ridge Mountains.

Bartram's *Travels* presents a similar mixture of styles and genres. Part travel narrative and part scientific inventory of Southern wildlife, it also reveals Bartram's Quaker sensibility regarding the spiritual dimension of nature, "that inexpressibly more essential principle which secretly operates within."

Lewis and Clark, meanwhile, led the expedition to explore the territory of the Louisiana Purchase of 1803, by which President Thomas Jefferson doubled the size of the United States. Their journals—written in very different voices by the literary Lewis and the laconic Clark—combine a host of styles and interests, from diary to field report, adventure narrative, and natural history essay. Taken as a whole, these writings present the most complete account of the pre-settlement prairies, mountains, deserts, and rivers of the West.

Antebellum Representations

Travel writing became a major vehicle for recording observations of the natural environment in nineteenth-century America. A bare list of authors and titles suggests the richness of these materials: Henry

Rowe Schoolcraft, *Journal of a Tour into the Interior of Missouri and Arkansaw* (1821); Timothy Dwight, *Travels in New England and New York* (1821–1822); Edwin James, *Account of an Expedition from Pittsburgh to the Rocky Mountains* (1822–1823); Washington Irving, *A Tour on the Prairies* (1835); John Kirk Townsend, *Narrative of a Journey Across the Rocky Mountains, to the Columbia River* (1839); Margaret Fuller, *Summer on the Lakes, in 1843* (1844); John C. Frémont and Jessie Benton Frémont, *Report of the Exploring Expedition to the Rocky Mountains in the Year 1842, and to Oregon and North California in 1843–1844* (1845); Henry David Thoreau, *A Week on the Concord and Merrimack Rivers* (1849); and Howard Stansbury, *Exploration and Survey of the Valley of the Great Salt Lake of Utah* (1852).

Many of these writers resemble one another in describing the vast American interior, its rich biological diversity, and the vulnerability of its native inhabitants—human and nonhuman—to the encroaching settlements. The attitudes toward nature in nineteenth-century travel writing range from hostile to romantic, from scientific to commercial. But it is well to remember that all of these writers, while American-born, were tourists and not settlers or native inhabitants.

Linguistic and cultural barriers operated to restrict the opportunities for Native Americans, African Americans, and women to publish their narratives. The restriction was especially acute in the case of Native Americans, whose culture was primarily oral and whose languages represented a formidable challenge to Anglo-American translators well into the twentieth century.

The work of Jane Johnston Schoolcraft (known as Bame-wa-was-ge-zhik-a-quay) and her husband, Henry Rowe Schoolcraft, is an important exception. Jane Johnston was an Ojibwa Indian who married the multitalented Schoolcraft in 1823; she collected and translated the bulk of the Ojibwa tales and legends that appear in Schoolcraft's popular book, *Algic Researches, Comprising Inquiries Respecting the Mental Characteristics of the North American Indians* (1839). The Schoolcrafts' Ojibwa tales reveal an animistic view of nature, in which the relationship between humans and nonhumans is mediated by language and moral codes. The narratives stress the collaboration between human beings and natural forces rather than the domination or possession of nature by humanity. The tales often express a kinship between the spiritual power of animals and the spiritual life of native communities.

The mainstream literary genres of fiction and poetry reveal a variety of attitudes toward the American environment, but a generally favorable view of nature arose as a direct result of the flowering of Romanticism in the late eighteenth and early nineteenth centuries. William Cullen Bryant's poems—such as "Thanatopsis" (1817), "To a Waterfowl" (1821), "A Forest Hymn" (1825), and "The Prairies" (1833)—are characteristic. Inspired by English Romantic poet William Wordsworth, Bryant expresses a calm assurance in the peaceful processes of nature.

Bryant's contemporary, James Fenimore Cooper, is famous for his Leatherstocking Tales. This series of five novels—*The Pioneers* (1823), *The Last of the Mohicans* (1826), *The Prairie* (1827), *The Pathfinder* (1840), and *The Deerslayer* (1841)—features the exploits of the frontier scout Natty Bumppo from his youth to death at an advanced age. As they move from the forests of New York state and Michigan to the high-grass prairies of the Middle West, Cooper's tales trace the settling of the continent and the conflicts between settlers and native inhabitants, giving epic scope to the history of westward expansion. Natty Bumppo combines the heroic qualities of epic literature and folktales, passing between the realms of civilization and nature, white culture and Native American culture, practical knowledge and sacred wisdom.

Parallel to the poetry of Bryant and the fiction of Cooper are the Romantic landscape paintings of the Hudson River School. Thomas Cole was the earliest and best-known painter of the group, but later artists such as Albert Bierstadt, Frederic Edwin Church, Asher B. Durand, and Thomas Moran continued the strain of romanticizing the American wilderness long past the Civil War. Their paintings emphasized the grandeur and sublimity of American nature, with the human figure often dwarfed by the scale of the surrounding landscape. Wilderness was awesome and dangerous, but it also suggested the religious and aesthetic dimensions beyond the purely material places.

Nature in the American Renaissance

Some of the greatest writers in American literary history were actively engaged in representing American nature during the final decade of the antebellum period. Nathaniel Hawthorne's stories and novels of

In his 1849 oil painting "Kindred Spirits," Asher Durand depicts
fellow Hudson River School artist Thomas Cole and poet
William Cullen Bryant in a romanticized wilderness setting.

Puritan New England do not exhaust his writing about nature. In
such later novels as *The House of the Seven Gables* (1851), *The Blithedale
Romance* (1852), and *The Marble Faun* (1860), Hawthorne repeatedly
meditated on the relationship between nature and the uses to which
human beings put it. In *The Blithedale Romance,* for example, a group
of visionary artists and social reformers attempt to live in a utopian
community modeled on the Transcendentalist social experiment
Brook Farm, but their pastoral imaginations only reveal the dark
secrets of their past identities.

Similar to Hawthorne in vision and genius, Herman Melville
explored the relationship between men and the sea in a number of

novels, most notably his whaling masterpiece, *Moby-Dick* (1851). The monomaniacal, vengeful hunt of Captain Ahab drives the narrative toward its tragic conclusion, in which the power of nature, embodied in the white whale, becomes truly marvelous. Hawthorne and Melville differed from other great writers of the mid-nineteenth century in their dark, prophetic gloom.

In essays and poems written over a long, productive life, Ralph Waldo Emerson established himself as the preeminent literary figure in antebellum America. Significantly, Emerson's first book was titled *Nature* (1836), in which he develops his Transcendentalist view of how nature and spirit relate to one another through poetic intuition and language. Emerson's optimistic, progressive view of temporal change and mortality was tempered in his later years, as recorded in the great essays "The Poet" and "Experience" (both 1844) and the poem "Threnody" (1847). But he remained committed to the view of nature as a symbol of spirit. In poems such as "Each and All," "Hamatreya," "The Snow-Storm," and "Woodnotes" (all 1847), he presents a dynamic, shifting vision of both nature and those who experience it.

Henry David Thoreau shared Emerson's fundamental notion of a transcendental reality, placing great faith in the flash of insight and the moment of union between nature and spirit. In *Walden; or, Life in the Woods* (1854), Thoreau developed his own version of Emersonian Transcendentalism, focusing on the relationship between his individual imagination and the local environment of Walden Pond and the woods around Concord, Massachusetts. The two years that Thoreau lived at Walden Pond—1845 to 1847—were not a retreat from civilization but an experiment in living in the middle ground between wild nature and cultivated nature.

During the Walden years, Thoreau made his first of three excursions to the northern forests of Maine, traveling to Mount Katahdin in September 1846. He returned in 1853 and 1857, resulting in the posthumous volume, *The Maine Woods* (1864). The book reveals Thoreau's intense interest in natural history, especially botany, and his desire to learn as much as possible about the native people of his region. Thoreau's transcendental vision ultimately is more concrete, specific, and earthy than Emerson's abstract and philosophical view. The result, referred to as the "environmental imagination," has led to continued interest in Thoreau's writing. His other essays about nature include "The Natural History of Massachusetts" (1842), "The

Succession of Forest Trees" (1860), and "Walking," "Autumnal Tints," and "Wild Apples" (all 1862).

Another important writer of nature during the period was Walt Whitman, whose *Leaves of Grass* (1855–1892) was a continually revised record of the poet's vision of transcendental union between nature and spirit. For Whitman, the soul or spirit was always in flux, always in motion; only in that way could it approach the moving power of the natural world. Whitman was fascinated by the agricultural and industrial uses to which Americans put the vast landscape they were settling, but he always returned to a solitary speaker, face-to-face with the awesome marvels of an impersonal environment. A reader finds many such moments in the masterpiece "Song of Myself" (1855); perhaps even better for revealing his variety of attitudes toward nature are such poems as "Out of the Cradle Endlessly Rocking" (1859), "As I Ebb'd with the Ocean of Life" (1860), and even "When Lilacs Last in the Dooryard Bloom'd" (1865).

In the early years of the American republic, then, nature was something that many Americans feared—large, mysterious, and dangerous. As explorers and frontier settlers began to conquer the vast wilderness, however, the unique qualities of the North American continent became an important part of the nation's identity, and the American landscape was celebrated in poetry, prose, and paintings. This trend would accelerate after the Civil War, particularly as "nature" began to disappear at a rapid rate in the face of population growth and industrial development.

James Perrin Warren

See also: Literature of the Early Republic; Bryant, William Cullen; Cooper, James Fenimore; Emerson, Ralph Waldo; Hawthorne, Nathaniel; Melville, Herman; Poetry; Thoreau, Henry David; Transcendentalism; Whittier, John Greenleaf

Equiano, Olaudah

(1745–1797)

In 1789, the English reading public had its first opportunity to read an account of slavery from the perspective of an African native who had been kidnapped from his tribe, transported across the ocean to America, and sold into bondage. His name was Olaudah Equiano, though he would also become known to English speakers by his slave name, Gustavus Vassa. His highly popular autobiography, *The Interesting Narrative of the Life of Olaudah Equiano or Gustavus Vassa, the African, Written by Himself*, was published in the United States two years later. Recognized as the first major work in the genre of the slave narrative, the book described the terror of his capture, the long nightmare of the transatlantic Middle Passage, the brutal and dehumanizing experience of slavery, and his eventual life as a freedman and antislavery advocate.

According to his own account, Equiano was born in 1745 as a member of the Ibo tribe in the prosperous farming village of Essaka (Isseke) in what is now Nigeria. At the age of 11, he was captured by slave traders along with his sister. After several months of travel, during which he was traded several times and separated from his sister, Equiano arrived on Africa's west coast and was sold to European slave traders. Enduring the horrors of the Middle Passage, he arrived on the island of Barbados and was promptly transferred to colonial Virginia, where he was sold to a tobacco planter named Campbell. In 1757, Michael Pascal, an English naval officer, purchased the 12-year-old and renamed him Gustavus Vassa after a sixteenth-century Swedish king.

Equiano accompanied Pascal on military campaigns in the French and Indian War, participating in the successful 1758 siege of Louisbourg, a French fortress on Canada's Cape Breton Island. Besides becoming a skilled sailor, Equiano learned to read and write and was baptized in

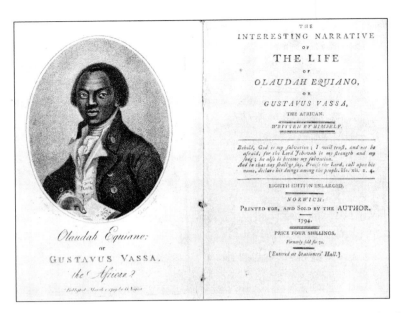

The popular autobiography of Olaudah Equiano, published in 1789, was the first major work in a defining genre of early American literature—the slave narrative.

the Church of England. In 1763, Pascal sold Equiano to Robert King, a Quaker slave trader living on Montserrat in the West Indies. King permitted Equiano not only to earn money but also to invest in trading voyages between the West Indies and Georgia and South Carolina. Within three years, he had earned enough to buy his freedom.

As a freedman, Equiano returned to London in 1768 and continued to travel for the next three decades. From the Arctic (where he participated in a quest to find a Northwest Passage) to Turkey, Genoa, Spain, Nicaragua, Pennsylvania, New York, and England, he saw much of the Atlantic and Mediterranean worlds, earning his livelihood as a hairdresser, merchant, personal servant, author, and lecturer.

Equiano's efforts on behalf of the antislavery movement came about relatively slowly. Indeed, he worked with Robert King in the slave trade for two years and, in the mid-1770s, worked as an overseer on a slave plantation in Nicaragua. The brutality he experienced and helped facilitate, along with a profound spiritual conversion in 1774, finally led Equiano to seek ways to ameliorate the condition of slaves and then to attack slavery and the slave trade.

After the Anglican Church rejected his offer to serve as a missionary to Africa in 1779, Equiano took up writing, lecturing, and other efforts on behalf of the abolitionist cause. He published letters and reviews critical of proslavery advocates, particularly West Indian planter James Tobin and his assertions of black inferiority. Equiano took part in a project to relocate poor blacks from London to Sierra Leone, and, in 1788, submitted an antislavery petition to King George III. Advocating interracial marriage as a solution to the multitude of problems associated with differences of color, Equiano set an example by marrying Susan Cullen, an Englishwoman, in 1792; the couple would have two daughters.

Yet it was his 1789 autobiography that made Equiano a truly influential figure in the antislavery crusade. Part spiritual narrative, part adventure tale, and part travel account, the *Interesting Narrative* above all was a powerful indictment of slavery and the slave trade, drawing upon his experiences as both a victim and, for a time, perpetrator of the pernicious labor system. For the next eight years, Equiano traveled throughout the British Isles, promoting the book and continuing his campaign against slavery. Going through eight editions in England alone, the *Interesting Narrative* was an enormous best seller and helped fuel the movement to end the English slave trade. The book soon appeared in five other nations, including the United States in 1791; it had the same stunning effect everywhere.

In addition to establishing Equiano as one of the most powerful voices against the transatlantic slave trade, his autobiography became the prototype of an important new literary genre in America, the slave narrative. By the time of the Civil War, more than a hundred of such accounts had appeared, the most notable of which was Frederick Douglass's classic *Narrative of the Life of Frederick Douglass* (1845). Describing the oppressive cruelty of bondage, such works stood as grim testimony to the yearning for freedom among slaves and to the inhumanity of perpetuating such a system.

Referring to himself as "the African," Equiano yearned to set foot in his homeland once more before dying but never had the opportunity. He died in London on March 31, 1797, at the age of 52. Britain abolished the slave trade ten years later and slavery itself in 1833.

Larry Gragg

◇◇

The Interesting Narrative of the Life of Olaudah Equiano (excerpt), 1789

◇◇

Kidnapped by slave traders from his Nigerian village at the age of 11, Olaudah Equiano was sold into slavery in colonial Virginia but eventually earned his freedom and devoted his life to abolishing the Atlantic slave trade. In this excerpt from his autobiography, The Interesting Narrative of the Life of Olaudah Equiano *(1789), Equiano describes his first glimpse of the Atlantic Ocean and the slave ship that will transport him away; the horrors of the Middle Passage; and the ship's arrival on the island of Barbados, where he and the other surviving human cargo are first put up for auction.*

The first object which saluted my eyes when I arrived on the coast was the sea, and a slave ship, which was then riding at anchor, and waiting for its cargo. These filled me with astonishment, which was soon converted into terror when I was carried on board. I was immediately handled and tossed up to see if I were sound by some of the crew; and I was now persuaded that I had gotten into a world of bad spirits, and that they were going to kill me. Their complexions too differing so much from ours, their long hair, and the language they spoke, (which was very different from any I had ever heard) united to confirm me in this belief. Indeed such were the horrors of my views and fears at the moment, that, if ten thousand worlds had been my own, I would have freely parted with them all to have exchanged my condition with that of the meanest slave in my own country. When I looked round the ship too and saw a large furnace or copper boiling, and a multitude of black people of every description chained together, every one of their countenances expressing dejection and sorrow, I no longer doubted of my fate; and, quite overpowered with horror and anguish, I fell motionless on the deck and fainted. When I recovered a little I found some black people about me, who I believed were some of those who brought me on board, and had been receiving their pay; they talked to me in order to cheer me, but all in vain. I asked them if we were not to be eaten by those white men with horrible looks, red faces, and loose hair. They told me I was not; and one of the crew brought me a small portion of spirituous liquor in a wine glass; but, being afraid of him, I would not take it out of his hand. One of the blacks therefore took it from him and gave it to me, and I took a little down my palate, which, instead of reviving me, as they thought it would, threw me into the greatest consternation at the strange feeling it produced, having never tasted any such liquor before. Soon after this the blacks who brought me on board went off, and left me abandoned to despair. I now saw myself deprived of all chance of returning to my native country, or even the least glimpse of hope of gaining the shore, which I now considered as friendly; and I even wished for my former slavery in preference to my present situation, which was filled with horrors of every kind, still heightened by my ignorance of what I was to undergo. I was not long suffered to indulge my grief; I was soon put down under the decks, and there I received such a salutation in my nostrils as I had never experienced in my life: so that, with the loathsomeness of the stench, and crying together, I became so sick and low that I was not able to eat, nor had I the least desire to taste any thing. I now wished for the last friend, death, to relieve me; but soon, to my grief, two of the white men offered me eatables; and, on my refusing to eat, one of them held me fast by the hands, and laid me across I think the windlass, and tied my feet, while the other flogged me severely. I had never experienced any thing of this kind before; and although, not being used to the water, I naturally feared that element the first time I saw it, yet nevertheless, could I have got over the nettings, I would have jumped over the side, but I could not; and, besides, the crew used to watch us very closely who were not chained down to the decks, lest we should leap into the water: and I have seen some of these poor African prisoners most severely cut for attempting to do so, and hourly whipped for not eating. This indeed was often the case with myself. In a little time after, amongst the poor chained men, I found some of my own nation, which in a small degree gave ease to my mind. I inquired of these what was to be done with us; they gave me to understand we were to be carried to these white people's country

> *I was soon put down under the decks, and there I received such a salutation in my nostrils as I had never experienced in my life.*

to work for them. I then was a little revived, and thought, if it were no worse than working, my situation was not so desperate: but still I feared I should be put to death, the white people looked and acted, as I thought, in so savage a manner; for I had never seen among any people such instances of brutal cruelty; and this not only shewn towards us blacks, but also to some of the whites themselves. One white man in particular I saw, when we were permitted to be on deck, flogged so unmercifully with a large rope near the foremast, that he died in consequence of it; and they tossed him over the side as they would have done a brute. This made me fear these people the more; and I expected nothing less than to be treated in the same manner. I could not help expressing my fears and apprehensions to some of my countrymen: I asked them if these people had no country, but lived in this hollow place (the ship): they told me they did not, but came from a distant one. 'Then,' said I, 'how comes it in all our country we never heard of them?' They told me because they lived so very far off. I then asked where were their women? had they any like themselves? I was told they had: 'and why,' said I, 'do we not see them?' they answered, because they were left behind. I asked how the vessel could go? they told me they could not tell; but that there were cloths put upon the masts by the help of the ropes I saw, and then the vessel went on; and the white men had some spell or magic they put in the water when they liked in order to stop the vessel. I was exceedingly amazed at this account, and really thought they were spirits. I therefore wished much to be from amongst them, for I expected they would sacrifice me: but my wishes were vain; for we were so quartered that it was impossible for any of us to make our escape. While we stayed on the coast I was mostly on deck; and one day, to my great astonishment, I saw one of these vessels coming in with the sails up. As soon as the whites saw it, they gave a great shout, at which we were amazed; and the more so as the vessel appeared larger by approaching nearer. At last she came to an anchor in my sight, and when the anchor was let go I and my countrymen who saw it were lost in astonishment to observe the vessel stop; and were not convinced it was done by magic. Soon after this the other ship got her boats out, and they came on board of us, and the people of both ships seemed very glad to see each other. Several of the strangers also shook hands with us black people, and made motions with their hands, signifying I suppose we were to go to their country; but we did not understand them. At last, when the ship we were in had got in all her cargo, they made ready with many fearful noises, and we were all put under deck, so that we could not see how they managed the vessel. But this disappointment was the least of my sorrow. The stench of the hold while we were on the coast was so intolerably loathsome, that it was dangerous to remain there for any time, and some of us had been permitted to stay on the deck for the fresh air; but now that the whole ship's cargo were confined together, it became absolutely pestilential. The closeness of the place, and the heat of the climate, added to the number in the ship, which was so crowded that each had scarcely room to turn himself, almost suffocated us. This produced copious perspirations, so that the air soon became unfit for respiration, from a variety of loathsome smells, and brought on a sickness among the slaves, of which many died, thus falling victims to the improvident avarice, as I may call it, of their purchasers. This wretched situation was again aggravated by the galling of the chains, now become insupportable; and the filth of the necessary tubs, into which the children often fell, and were almost suffocated. The shrieks of the women, and the groans of the dying, rendered the whole a scene of horror almost inconceivable. Happily perhaps for myself I was soon reduced so low here that it was thought necessary to keep me almost always on deck; and from my extreme youth I was not put in fetters. In this situation I expected every hour to share the fate of my companions, some of whom were almost daily brought upon deck at the point of death, which I began to hope would soon put an end to my miseries. Often did I think many of the inhabitants of the deep much more happy than myself. I envied them the freedom they enjoyed, and as often wished I could change my condition for theirs. Every circumstance I met with served only to render my state more painful, and heighten my apprehensions, and my opinion of the cruelty of the whites. One day they had taken a number of fishes; and when they had killed and satisfied themselves with as many as they thought fit, to our astonishment who were on the deck, rather than give any of them to us to eat as we expected, they tossed the remaining fish into the sea again, although we begged and prayed for some as well as we could, but in vain; and some of my countrymen, being pressed by hunger, took an opportunity, when they thought no one saw them, of trying to get a little privately; but they were discovered, and the attempt procured them some very severe floggings. One day, when we had a smooth sea and moderate wind, two of my wearied countrymen who were chained together (I was near them at the time), preferring death to such a life of misery, somehow made through the nettings and jumped into the sea: immediately another quite dejected fellow, who, on account of his illness, was suffered to be out of irons, also followed their example; and I believe many more would very soon have done the same if they had not been prevented by the ship's crew, who were instantly alarmed. Those of us that were the most active were in a moment put down under the deck, and there was such a noise and confusion amongst the people of the ship as I never heard before, to stop her, and get the boat out to go after the slaves. However two of the wretches were drowned, but they got the other, and afterwards flogged him unmercifully for thus attempting to prefer death to slavery. In this manner we continued to undergo more hardships than I can now relate, hardships which are inseparable from this accursed trade. Many a time we were near suffocation from the want of fresh air, which we were often without for whole days together. This, and the stench of the necessary tubs, carried off many. During our passage I first saw flying fishes, which surprised me very much: they used frequently to fly across the ship, and many of them fell on the deck. I also now first saw the use of the quadrant; I had often with astonishment seen the mariners make observations with it, and I could not think what it meant. They at last took notice of my surprise; and one of them, willing to increase it, as well as to gratify my curiosity, made me one day look through it. The clouds appeared to me to be land, which disappeared as they passed along. This heightened my wonder; and I was now more persuaded than ever that I was in another world, and that every thing about me was magic. At last we came in sight of the island of Barbadoes, at which the whites on board gave a great shout, and made many signs of joy to us. We did not know what to think of this; but as the vessel drew nearer we plainly saw the harbour, and other ships of different kinds and sizes; and we soon anchored amongst them off Bridge Town. Many merchants and planters now came on board, though it was in the evening. They put us in separate parcels, and examined us attentively. They also made us jump, and pointed to the land, signifying we were to go there. We thought by this we should be eaten by these ugly men, as they appeared to us; and, when soon after we were all put down under the deck again, there was much dread and trembling among us, and nothing but bitter cries to be heard all the night from these apprehensions, insomuch that at last the white people got some old slaves from the land to pacify us. They told us we were not to be eaten, but to work, and were soon to go on land, where we should see many of our country people. This report eased us much; and sure enough, soon after we were landed, there came to us Africans of all languages. We were conducted immediately to the merchant's yard, where we were all pent up together like so many sheep in a fold, without regard to sex or age. As every object was new to me every thing I saw filled me with surprise. What struck me first was that the houses were built with stories, and in every other respect different from those in Africa: but I was still more astonished on seeing people on horseback. I did not know what this could mean; and indeed I thought these people were full of nothing but magical arts. While I was in this aston-ishment one of my fellow prisoners spoke to a countryman of his about the horses, who said they were the same kind they had in their country. I understood them, though they were from a distant part of Africa, and I thought it odd I had not seen any horses there; but afterwards, when I came to converse with different Africans, I found they had many horses amongst them, and much larger than those I then saw. We were not many days in the merchant's custody before we were sold after their usual manner, which is this:—On a signal given, (as the beat of a drum) the buyers rush at once into the yard where the slaves are confined, and make choice of that parcel they like best. The noise and clamour with which this is attended, and the eagerness visible in the countenances of the buyers, serve not a little to increase the apprehensions of the terrified Africans, who may well be supposed to consider them as the ministers of that destruction to which they think themselves devoted. In this manner, without scruple, are relations and friends separated, most of them never to see each other again. I remember in the vessel in which I was brought over, in the men's apartment, there were several brothers, who, in the sale, were sold in different lots; and it was very moving on this occasion to see and hear their cries at parting. O, ye nominal Christians! might not an African ask you, learned you this from your God, who says unto you, Do unto all men as you would men should do unto you? Is it not enough that we are torn from our country and friends to toil for your luxury and lust of gain? Must every tender feeling be likewise sacrificed to your avarice? Are the dearest friends and relations, now rendered more dear by their separation from their kindred, still to be parted from each other, and thus prevented from cheering the gloom of slavery with the small comfort of being together and mingling their sufferings and sorrows? Why are parents to lose their children, brothers their sisters, or husbands their wives? Surely this is a new refinement in cruelty, which, while it has no advantage to atone for it, thus aggravates distress, and adds fresh horrors even to the wretchedness of slavery.

Source: Paul Edwards, ed., *The Life of Olaudah Equiano or Gustavus Vassa, The African* (1789), 2 vols. (London: Dawsons of Pall Mall, 1969).

Fuller, Margaret
(1810–1850)

Author, journalist, teacher, feminist, and literary and social critic
Sarah Margaret Fuller was one of antebellum America's foremost intellectuals. She is best known as the author of *Woman in the Nineteenth
Century* (1845), for her pioneering advocacy of women's rights and
social reforms, and for her role in the Transcendentalist movement.
She has been called America's first major woman author and journalist, as well as the most influential gender theorist of her time.

Fuller was born in Cambridgeport (present-day Cambridge), Massachusetts, on May 23, 1810. Her father, Timothy Fuller, Jr., was a lawyer
and politician who served in the Massachusetts Senate and the U.S.
Congress. A Jeffersonian Democrat and Unitarian, he demanded of his
eldest daughter hard work and intellectual discipline. Fuller's mother,
Margaret Crane, evoked what her famous daughter later described as
the Muse-like qualities of emotion, intuition, and spirituality.

By the age of 16, Fuller's remarkable intellect and forceful personal-
ity had garnered attention and, occasionally, criticism. At a time when
female education was supposed to prepare girls for marriage and
motherhood, Fuller's schooling was grounded in the classics and in Enlightenment principles. Her conversational style, even at a young age,
was described as commanding, somewhat judgmental, and sprinkled
with topics that challenged the status quo. Devoted to self-cultivation,
Fuller studied literature, philosophy, and languages; by adulthood,
she was fluent in Latin, Greek, French, Italian, and German.

With his political career in decline, Timothy Fuller in 1833 relocated the
family to the country town of Groton, Massachusetts, so that he might
pursue the life of a farmer-scholar in the mold of Thomas Jefferson. He
died two years later, however, leaving the family in difficult financial
straits. To help support her mother and younger siblings, Margaret
Fuller began teaching. She first taught in Boston with the controversial

and innovative educator Amos Bronson Alcott at his Temple School, and then at the Greene Street School in Providence, Rhode Island.

In 1839, Fuller moved her family to Jamaica Plain, near Boston, where she became known as a "conversationalist," moderating small group discussions on a variety of intellectual and philosophical topics. These conversation groups were sufficiently profitable to allow her to undertake translations of several notable works of German literature, which were well received. Based on these group discussions—which included such leaders of the early feminist movement as Lydia Maria Child and Julia Ward Howe—Fuller also produced her most important work, *Woman in the Nineteenth Century* (1845). Astonishingly modern in its assertion that women's lives must be powerful and complete rather than stunted by artificial social and cultural constraints, the book envisioned an ideal of egalitarian human development and human relationships.

During this period, Fuller also published several literary essays and developed an active correspondence and friendship with the philosopher and essayist Ralph Waldo Emerson. The latter introduced her to a network of intellectuals who, like herself, were critical of traditional religion and frustrated with the growing materialism and social inequities in the industrializing Northeast. When a group of these Transcendentalists began publishing *The Dial* in midsummer 1840, Fuller accepted a two-year appointment as its editor. She also contributed many of her own literary reviews and essays to the journal. Emerson extolled her "sincerity, force, & fluency as a writer."

Horace Greeley, the renowned editor of the *New York Tribune*, hired Fuller in late 1844 as the paper's literary critic—making her the first such columnist for any American newspaper. She relocated to New York City, where she became more directly involved in reform movements concerning slavery, women's rights, prostitution, and prison conditions. From the end of 1845 to her untimely death in 1850, Fuller published some 250 articles advocating prison reform; decrying the treatment of Irish immigrants, American Indians, slaves, prostitutes, and the working poor; and condemning the underlying social conditions that oppressed these groups.

As the *Tribune*'s foreign correspondent, Fuller traveled to Europe in 1846, where she was welcomed by such literary giants as Thomas Carlyle, George Sand, and William Wordsworth. She also forged a friendship with the exiled Italian revolutionary Giuseppe Mazzini.

Author, journalist, and literary critic Margaret Fuller was a central figure in the Transcendentalist movement and a pioneer of the women's rights movement in America.

During the Italian Revolution of 1848, while filing reports for the *Tribune*, Fuller urged Americans to learn the real meaning of fraternity and equality from the struggles of the working classes.

While in Rome, she met, fell in love with, and probably married the young aristocrat Giovanni Angelo Ossoli. Together they had a son, Angelo. In February 1849, Fuller and Ossoli celebrated the rise of an independent Roman republic and hoped for a peaceful, socialist revolution to spread throughout Europe; five months later, the republic fell. In summer 1850, while at work on a history of the Italian Revolution, Fuller embarked with her family for the United States. All three perished when their ship wrecked in a hurricane off the coast of New York on July 19.

Margaret Fuller had an enduring influence as a pioneering feminist, an influential Transcendentalist, and a social reformer who was not afraid to unmask class, race, and gender injustices. In their *History of Woman Suffrage* (1881–1902), the famed suffragists Susan B. Anthony and Elizabeth Cady Stanton wrote that Fuller "possessed more influence on the thought of American women than any woman previous to her time."

Cynthia M. Kennedy and Barbara Schwarz Wachal

See also: Emerson, Ralph Waldo; Transcendentalism

◇◇

Woman in the Nineteenth Century (excerpt), 1845

◇◇

Margaret Fuller's pioneering work of the feminist movement had its first itera-tion in an article titled "The Great Lawsuit. Man versus Men. Woman versus Women," which appeared in the July 1843 issue of the Transcendentalist jour-nal The Dial, *then edited by Ralph Waldo Emerson. An expanded version was published in book form two years later, as* Woman in the Nineteenth Century. *Invoking an androgynous ideal from ancient mythology, Fuller argues that all people embody the "feminine" qualities of the Muse—mystical, creative, intuitive powers—as well as the "masculine" energy, practicality, and intel-lectual vigor of Minerva. Only when these complementary elements are fully developed, Fuller maintains, will women and men experience complete and harmonious lives. In the passage that follows, she goes on to advocate freedom and equality for women in every sphere of public and domestic life.*

. . . I have aimed to show that no age was left entirely without a witness of the equality of the sexes in function, duty and hope.

Also that, when there was unwillingness or ignorance, which prevented this being acted upon, women had not the less power for their want of light and noble freedom. But it was power which hurt alike them and those against whom they made use of the arms of the servile,—cunning, blandishment, and unreasonable emotion.

That now the time has come when a clearer vision and better action are possible—when Man and Woman may regard one another, as brother and sister, the pillars of one porch, the priests of one worship.

I have believed and intimated that this hope would receive an ampler fruition, than ever before, in our own land.

And it will do so if this land carry out the principles from which sprang our national life.

I believe that, at present, women are the best helpers of one another.

Let them think; let them act; till they know what they need.

We only ask of men to remove arbitrary barriers. Some would like to do more. But I believe it needs that Woman show herself in her native dignity, to teach them how to aid her; their minds are so encumbered by tradition. . . .

You ask, what use will she make of liberty, when she has so long been sustained and restrained?

I answer; in the first place, this will not be suddenly given. I read yesterday a debate of this year on the subject of enlarging women's rights over property. It was a leaf from the class-book that is preparing for the needed instruction. The men learned visibly as they spoke. The champions of Woman saw the fallacy of arguments on the opposite side, and were startled by their own convictions. With their wives at home, and the readers of the paper, it was the same. And so the stream flows on; thought urging action, and action leading to the evolution of still better thought.

But, were this freedom to come suddenly, I have no fear of the consequences. Individuals might commit excesses, but there is not only in the sex a reverence for decorums and limits inherited and enhanced from generation to generation, which many years of other life could not efface, but a native love, in Woman as Woman, of proportion, of "the simple art of not too much,"—a Greek moderation, which would create immediately a restraining party, the natural legislators and instructors of the rest, and would gradually establish such rules as are needed to guard, without impeding, life.

The Graces would lead the choral dance, and teach the rest to regulate their steps to the measure of beauty.

But if you ask me what offices they may fill, I reply—any. I do not care what case you put; let them be sea-captains, if you will. I do not doubt there are women well fitted for such an office, and, if so, I should be as glad to see them in it, as to welcome the maid of Saragossa, or the maid of Missolonghi, or the Suliote heroine, or Emily Plater.

I think women need, especially at this juncture, a much greater range of occupation than they have, to rouse their latent powers. A party of travellers lately visited a lonely hut on a mountain. There they found an old woman, who told them she and her husband had lived there forty years. "Why," they said, "did you choose so barren a spot?" She "did not know; *it was the man's notion.*"

> *The Graces would lead the choral dance, and teach the rest to regulate their steps to the measure of beauty.*

And, during forty years, she had been content to act, without knowing why, upon "the man's notion." I would not have it so.

In families that I know, some little girls like to saw wood, others to use carpenters' tools. Where these tastes are indulged, cheerfulness and good-humor are promoted. Where they are forbidden, because "such things are not proper for girls," they grow sullen and mischievous.

Fourier had observed these wants of women, as no one can fail to do who watches the desires of little girls, or knows the ennui that haunts grown women, except where they make to themselves a serene little world by art of some kind. He, therefore, in proposing a great variety of employments, in manufactures or the care of plants and animals, allows for one third of women as likely to have a taste for masculine pursuits, one third of men for feminine.

Who does not observe the immediate glow and serenity that is diffused over the life of women, before restless or fretful, by engaging in gardening, building, or the lowest department of art? Here is something that is not routine, something that draws forth life towards the infinite.

I have no doubt, however, that a large proportion of women would give themselves to the same employments as now, because there are circumstances that must lead them. Mothers will delight to make the nest soft and warm. Nature would take care of that; no need to clip the wings of any bird that wants to soar and sing, or finds in itself the strength of pinion for a migratory flight unusual to its kind. The difference would be that *all* need not be constrained to employments for which *some* are unfit.

I have urged upon the sex self-subsistence in its two forms of self-reliance and self-impulse, because I believe them to be the needed means of the present juncture.

I have urged on Woman independence of Man, not that I do not think the sexes mutually needed by one another, but because in Woman this fact has led to an excessive devotion, which has cooled love, degraded marriage, and prevented either sex from being what it should be to itself or the other.

I wish Woman to live, *first* for God's sake. Then she will not make an imperfect man her god, and thus sink to idolatry. Then she will not take what is not fit for her from a sense of weakness and poverty. Then, if she finds what she needs in Man embodied, she will know how to love, and be worthy of being loved.

By being more a soul, she will not be less Woman, for nature is perfected through spirit.

Now there is no woman, only an overgrown child. . . .

A profound thinker has said, "No married woman can represent the female world, for she belongs to her husband. The idea of Woman must be represented by a virgin."

But that is the very fault of marriage, and of the present relation between the sexes, that the woman does belong to the man, instead of forming a whole with him. Were it otherwise, there would be no such limitation to the thought.

Woman, self-centred, would never be absorbed by any relation; it would be only an experience to her as to man. It is a vulgar error that love, *a* love, to Woman is her whole existence; she also is born for Truth and Love in their universal energy. . . .

An idea not unknown to ancient times has of late been revived, that, in the metamorphoses of life, the soul assumes the form, first of Man, then of Woman, and takes the chances, and reaps the benefits of either lot. Why then, say some, lay such emphasis on the rights or needs of Woman? What she wins not as Woman will come to her as Man.

That makes no difference. It is not Woman, but the law of right, the law of growth, that speaks in us, and demands the perfection of each being in its kind—apple as apple, Woman as Woman. Without adopting your theory, I know that I, a daughter, live through the life of Man; but what concerns me now is, that my life be a beautiful, powerful, in a word, a complete life in its kind. Had I but one more moment to live I must wish the same.

Source: S. Margaret Fuller, *Woman in the Nineteenth Century* (New York: Greeley & McElrath, 1845).

Hawthorne, Nathaniel

(1804–1864)

The fact that novelist and short-story writer Nathaniel Hawthorne was born on Independence Day adds a serendipitous detail to his status as one of the most pioneering and influential of all early American writers. His works, while written mostly in the vague, "misty" style of European romances, nonetheless contributed to the creation of a distinctly American literature, drawing heavily on the country's Puritan past and set primarily in Hawthorne's native New England. His two acknowledged masterworks of long fiction, *The Scarlet Letter* (1850) and *The House of the Seven Gables* (1851), probed the murky psychological side of sixteenth-century Massachusetts society, specifically the dark impulses beating beneath a veneer of righteousness and civility. Despite grappling with the complexities of guilt and sin, revolution and independence, utopian visions, and other cultural realities of early America, Hawthorne regarded writing as a "pleasurable toil."

Early Life and First Writings

Hawthorne was born on July 4, 1804, in Salem, Massachusetts. His father, Nathaniel Hathorne, was a sea captain who died of yellow fever in Dutch Guiana when the boy was only four. Hawthorne's childhood was divided between Salem and his mother's family home in Maine. He was a voracious reader, poring through the works of British authors such as Henry Fielding, William Godwin, Sir Walter Scott, and Horace Walpole. Hawthorne's great-great-grandfather, John Hathorne, had been one of the magistrates who presided over the Salem witch trials of 1692. As a young man, Hawthorne added the "w" to his surname to distance himself from the dark past of his Puritan forebears.

Financially supported by his maternal uncles, Hawthorne attended Bowdoin College in Maine, graduating in 1825. While at Bowdoin, he was a classmate of poet Henry Wadsworth Longfellow and a friend of future president Franklin Pierce. Upon graduation, Hawthorne returned home to Salem, where he devoted himself for the next several years to writing—largely in isolation. During this time, he footed the cost of anonymously publishing his first novel, *Fanshawe* (1828), which proved to be neither a critical nor a commercial success. He also contributed a number of short stories to various magazines and journals. These were collected and published in 1837 as the first volume of his *Twice-Told Tales*, the title of which Hawthorne took from Shakespeare's *King John:* "Life is as tedious as a twice-told tale / Vexing the dull eare of a drowsie man." Having received a copy of *Twice-Told Tales* from Hawthorne, Longfellow praised the volume in the *North American Review,* the first literary magazine in the United States. Edgar Allan Poe, however, took exception to Hawthorne's use of allegory, indirect symbolism, and heavy-handed moralizing. Hawthorne published a second volume of *Twice-Told Tales* five years later.

In 1839, Hawthorne accepted a political appointment to the Boston Custom House, where he worked for a year as a "weighter and gauger" to help support his writing. In 1841, he lived for a short time at Brook Farm, a Transcendentalist utopian community in West Roxbury, Massachusetts. Hawthorne would later develop his experiences in West Roxbury into a novel, *The Blithedale Romance* (1852), which featured a commune setting based on Brook Farm.

Concord, Lenox, and Major Works

Hawthorne was married to the artist Sophia Peabody in 1842, and the couple moved shortly thereafter to Concord, Massachusetts. In Concord, they rented a house called "Old Manse" from the family of essayist Ralph Waldo Emerson. The Hawthornes became intimately involved in the social circle of the New England Transcendentalists, which included Emerson, Bronson Alcott, and Henry David Thoreau. It was during this time that Hawthorne wrote most of the stories that were later collected in *Mosses from an Old Manse* (1846), including such now-famous tales as "The Old Manse," "The Birth-mark," "Young Goodman Brown," "Rappaccini's Daughter," and the innovative "P.'s

In such Romantic novels as *The Scarlet Letter* and *The House of the Seven Gables*—American classics—Nathaniel Hawthorne looked back on the dark side of Puritan society.

Correspondence," one of the first examples of the alternative history genre. One reader who was particularly influenced by *Mosses from an Old Manse* was Herman Melville, who wrote a favorable review of the collection. Melville and Hawthorne eventually became close friends and correspondents.

In 1846, again appointed as a customs official by the Democratic Party, Hawthorne and his family returned to Salem. But the presidential election of 1848, in which Whig Zachary Taylor replaced Democrat James K. Polk, resulted in Hawthorne's dismissal. He moved the family to Lenox in the Berkshire Mountains of Massachusetts, where he became part of a lively literary and social circle that came to include Melville, then writing *Moby-Dick* (1851). Melville, 15 years his junior, dedicated the novel to Hawthorne "in token of my admiration of his genius."

It was from Lenox that Hawthorne published, in quick succession, *The Scarlet Letter, The House of the Seven Gables,* and *The Blithedale*

Romance—the works in which his characteristic blend of shadowy romance and realistic detail reached its peak. *The Scarlet Letter,* in particular, went on to become one of the most widely read novels in American literature. Hawthorne published the volume with a preface that referenced his time as a surveyor at the Salem Custom House, suggesting that he had found documents there lending historical credibility to his fictional account.

In *The House of the Seven Gables,* Hawthorne told the story of the cursed Pyncheon family, displaying his intense Puritan interest in the sins and secrets that haunt old families, as well as his intellectual curiosity regarding the old mansions that dotted New England towns. Many years earlier, during the summer of 1837, Hawthorne had visited the town of Gardiner, Maine, and in his journal recorded his observations about the Gardiner family's run-down mansion. According to Hawthorne, such dwellings manifested "the indulgence of aristocratic pomp among democratic institutions," a distinctively American preoccupation that would form the focus of *The House of the Seven Gables.*

In the midst of this, his most productive period, Hawthorne also published another collection of short stories, *The Snow-Image and Other Twice-Told Tales* (1851), as well as two volumes of children's stories, *A Wonder Book* (1852) and *Tanglewood Tales* (1853).

Later Years

Inasmuch as he oscillated between periods of private creativity and public engagement, the next several years brought a decline in Hawthorne's productivity, as his life took a noticeably more political turn. For the 1852 presidential campaign, he wrote and published a biography of his college friend, Franklin Pierce, who subsequently won the election. After taking office, Pierce appointed Hawthorne as U.S. consul in Liverpool, England. The author and his family moved to Britain, where he carried out his diplomatic responsibilities until 1857. The Hawthornes then took an extended leave in Europe, traveling and living in Italy, France, and England, before returning to Concord in 1860.

Upon his return to Massachusetts, Hawthorne published his final novel, *The Marble Faun: or, The Romance of Monte Beni* (1860), which he had begun in Florence two years earlier. A kind of Gothic murder-mystery fable about expatriate American artists in Rome, *The Marble Faun* was well received by critics. After its publication, however, Hawthorne's health began to deteriorate. As his physical and creative energy waned during the final years of his life, he worked on several other long romances, none of which he completed, and kept copious notebooks that were published posthumously. He died in his sleep on May 19, 1864, while on a walking tour of the White Mountains of New Hampshire with former president Pierce. Like several of the Transcendentalists with whom he kept company—but whose bright optimism he rejected—Hawthorne was buried at the Sleepy Hollow Cemetery in Concord, near the Old Manse.

Corey McEleney

See also: Emerson, Ralph Waldo; Environment and Nature, Views of; Melville, Herman; Transcendentalism

Chapter Two, "The Market-Place," *The Scarlet Letter,* 1850

One of America's first writers of historical fiction, Nathaniel Hawthorne turned to Puritan Massachusetts of the 1640s for the setting of his 1850 Romantic novel and masterpiece The Scarlet Letter. *In his characteristically dark, allegorical style, Hawthorne tells the story of Hester Prynne, who conceives a daughter from an adulterous affair and must wear the red letter "A" on her dress as a badge of shame. The father of the child, the Reverend Arthur Dimmesdale, remains silent about his relationship with the young woman. Prynne's estranged husband, Roger Chillingworth, returns to the scene, suspects Dimmesdale, and torments him until forcing a public confession. In a reversal of conventional morality, however, the young adulterers are portrayed sympathetically, while Chillingworth is characterized as the true villain for having "violated, in cold blood, the sanctity of a human heart" (Dimmesdale's).*

Aside from the central themes of sin, guilt, hypocrisy, and redemption, The Scarlet Letter *alludes to an underlying conflict between the Puritan past and Hawthorne's personal present. On the one hand, he casts the moral rigidity, intolerance, and lack of humanity of the Puritans in a harsh light. On the other hand, he acknowledges that these same "bitter prosecutors" are his own "dim and dusty" ancestors. As in many of Hawthorne's other writings, one has the sense of the author's struggle with ancestral guilt and the evil in the human soul.*

In Chapter Two, reproduced here, Hester Prynne emerges from the prison where she has been held for the crime of adultery and enters the town square carrying her baby. With the letter "A" embroidered on her gown, she faces a spectacle of public condemnation and ridicule. Thus Hawthorne introduces both the main character and central themes of his novel. Prynne, a "figure of perfect elegance on a large scale," is believed to be modeled after Hawthorne's wife, Sophia.

II. The Market-Place

The grass-plot before the jail, in Prison Lane, on a certain summer morning, not less than two centuries ago, was occupied by a pretty large number of the inhabitants of Boston, all with their eyes intently fastened on the iron-clamped oaken door. Amongst any other population, or at a later period in the history of New England, the grim rigidity that petrified the bearded physiognomies of these good people would have augured some awful business in hand. It could have betokened nothing short of the anticipated execution of some noted culprit, on whom the sentence of a legal tribunal had but confirmed the verdict of public sentiment. But, in that early severity of the Puritan character, an inference of this kind could not so indubitably be drawn. It might be that a sluggish bond-servant, or an undutiful child, whom his parents had given over to the civil authority, was to be corrected at the whipping-post. It might be that an Antinomian, a Quaker, or other heterodox religionist, was to be scourged out of the town, or an idle or vagrant Indian, whom the white man's firewater had made riotous about the streets, was to be driven with stripes into the shadow of the forest. It might be, too, that a witch, like old Mistress Hibbins, the bitter-tempered widow of the magistrate, was to die upon the gallows. In either case, there was very much the same solemnity of demeanour on the part of the spectators, as befitted a people among whom religion and law were almost identical, and in whose character both were so thoroughly interfused, that the mildest and severest acts of public discipline were alike made venerable and awful. Meagre, indeed, and cold, was the sympathy that a transgressor might look for, from such bystanders, at the scaffold. On the other hand, a penalty which, in our days, would infer a degree of mocking infamy and ridicule, might then be invested with almost as stern a dignity as the punishment of death itself.

It was a circumstance to be noted on the summer morning when our story begins its course, that the women, of whom there were several in the crowd, appeared to take a peculiar interest in whatever penal infliction might be expected to ensue. The age had not so much refinement, that any sense of impropriety restrained the wearers of petticoat and farthingale from stepping forth into the public ways, and wedging their not unsubstantial persons, if occasion were, into the throng nearest to the scaffold at an execution. Morally, as well as materially, there was a coarser fibre in those wives and maidens of old English birth and breeding than in their fair descendants, separated from them by a series of six or seven generations; for, throughout that chain of ancestry, every successive mother had transmitted to her child a fainter bloom, a more delicate and briefer beauty, and a slighter physical frame, if not character of less force and solidity than her own. The women who were now standing about the prison-door stood within less than half a century of the period when the man-like Elizabeth had been the not altogether unsuitable representative of the sex. They were her countrywomen: and the beef and ale of their native land, with a moral diet not a whit more refined, entered largely into their composition. The bright morning sun, therefore, shone on broad shoulders and well-developed busts, and on round and ruddy cheeks, that had ripened in the far-off island, and had hardly yet grown paler or thinner in the atmosphere of New England. There was, moreover, a boldness and rotundity of speech among these matrons, as most of them seemed to be, that would startle us at the present day, whether in respect to its purport or its volume of tone.

"Goodwives," said a hard-featured dame of fifty, "I'll tell ye a piece of my mind. It would be greatly for the public behoof if we women, being of mature age and church-members in good repute, should have the handling of such malefactresses as this Hester Prynne. What think ye, gossips? If the hussy stood up for judgment before us five, that are now here in a knot together, would she come off with such a sentence as the worshipful magistrates have awarded? Marry, I trow not."

"People say," said another, "that the Reverend Master Dimmesdale, her godly pastor, takes it very grievously to heart that such a scandal should have come upon his congregation."

"The magistrates are God-fearing gentlemen, but merciful overmuch—that is a truth," added a third autumnal matron. "At the very least, they should have put the brand of a hot iron on Hester Prynne's forehead. Madame Hester would have winced at that, I warrant me. But she—the naughty baggage—little will she care what they put upon the bodice of her gown! Why, look you, she may cover it with a brooch, or such like heathenish adornment, and so walk the streets as brave as ever!"

"Ah, but," interposed, more softly, a young wife, holding a child by the hand, "let her cover the mark as she will, the pang of it will be always in her heart."

"What do we talk of marks and brands, whether on the bodice of her gown or the flesh of her forehead?" cried another female, the ugliest as well as the most pitiless of these self-constituted judges. "This woman has brought shame upon us all, and ought to die; is there not law for it? Truly there is, both in the Scripture and the statute-book. Then let the magistrates, who have made it of no effect, thank themselves if their own wives and daughters go astray."

"Mercy on us, goodwife!" exclaimed a man in the crowd, "is there no virtue in woman, save what springs from a wholesome fear of the gallows? That is the hardest word yet! Hush now, gossips for the lock is turning in the prison-door, and here comes Mistress Prynne herself."

The door of the jail being flung open from within there appeared, in the first place, like a black shadow emerging into sunshine, the grim and gristly presence of the town-beadle, with a sword by his side, and his staff of office in his hand. This personage prefigured and represented in his aspect the whole dismal

"This woman has brought shame upon us all. . . ."

severity of the Puritanic code of law, which it was his business to administer in its final and closest application to the offender. Stretching forth the official staff in his left hand, he laid his right upon the shoulder of a young woman, whom he thus drew forward, until, on the threshold of the prison-door, she repelled him, by an action marked with natural dignity and force of character, and stepped into the open air as if by her own free will. She bore in her arms a child, a baby of some three months old, who winked and turned aside its little face from the too vivid light of day; because its existence, heretofore, had brought it acquaintance only with the grey twilight of a dungeon, or other darksome apartment of the prison.

When the young woman—the mother of this child—stood fully revealed before the crowd, it seemed to be her first impulse to clasp the infant closely to her bosom; not so much by an impulse of motherly affection, as that she might thereby conceal a certain token, which was wrought or fastened into her dress. In a moment, however, wisely judging that one token of her shame would but poorly serve to hide another, she took the baby on her arm, and with a burning blush, and yet a haughty smile, and a glance that would not be abashed, looked around at her townspeople and neighbours. On the breast of her gown, in fine red cloth, surrounded with an elaborate embroidery and fantastic flourishes of gold thread, appeared the letter A. It was so artistically done, and with so much fertility and gorgeous luxuriance of fancy, that it had all the effect of a last and fitting decoration to the apparel which she wore, and which was of a splendour in accordance with the taste of the age, but greatly beyond what was allowed by the sumptuary regulations of the colony.

The young woman was tall, with a figure of perfect elegance on a large scale. She had dark and abundant hair, so glossy that it threw off the sunshine with a gleam; and a face which, besides being beautiful from regularity of feature and richness of complexion, had the impressiveness belonging to a marked brow and deep black eyes. She was ladylike, too, after the manner of the feminine gentility of those days; characterised by a certain state and dignity, rather than by the delicate, evanescent, and indescribable grace which is now recognised as its indication. And never had Hester Prynne appeared more ladylike, in the antique interpretation of the term, than as she issued from the prison. Those who had before known her, and had expected to behold her dimmed and obscured by a disastrous cloud, were astonished, and even startled, to perceive how her beauty shone out, and made a halo of the misfortune and ignominy in which she was enveloped. It may be true that, to a sensitive observer, there was some thing exquisitely painful in it. Her attire, which indeed, she had wrought for the occasion in prison, and had modelled much after her own fancy, seemed to express the attitude of her spirit, the desperate recklessness of her mood, by its wild and picturesque peculiarity. But the point which drew all eyes, and, as it were, transfigured the wearer—so that both men and women who had been familiarly acquainted with Hester Prynne were now impressed as if they beheld her for the first time— was that SCARLET LETTER, so fantastically embroidered and illuminated upon her bosom. It had the effect of a spell, taking her out of the ordinary relations with humanity, and enclosing her in a sphere by herself.

"She hath good skill at her needle, that's certain," remarked one of her female spectators; "but did ever a woman, before this brazen hussy, contrive such a way of showing it? Why, gossips, what is it but to laugh in the faces of our godly magistrates, and make a pride out of what they, worthy gentlemen, meant for a punishment?"

"It were well," muttered the most iron-visaged of the old dames, "if we stripped Madame Hester's rich gown off her dainty shoulders; and as for the red letter which she hath stitched so curiously, I'll bestow a rag of mine own rheumatic flannel to make a fitter one!"

"Oh, peace, neighbours—peace!" whispered their youngest companion; "do not let her hear you! Not a stitch in that embroidered letter but she has felt it in her heart."

The grim beadle now made a gesture with his staff. "Make way, good people—make way, in the King's name!" cried he. "Open a passage; and I promise ye, Mistress Prynne shall be set where man, woman, and child may have a fair sight of her brave apparel from this time till an hour past meridian. A blessing on the righteous colony of the Massachusetts, where iniquity is dragged out into the sunshine! Come along, Madame Hester, and show your scarlet letter in the market-place!"

A lane was forthwith opened through the crowd of spectators. Preceded by the beadle, and attended by an irregular procession of stern-browed men and unkindly visaged women, Hester Prynne set forth towards the place appointed for her punishment. A crowd of eager and curious schoolboys, understanding little of the matter in hand, except that it gave them a half-holiday, ran before her progress, turning their heads continually to stare into her face and at the winking baby in her arms, and at the ignominious letter on her breast. It was no great distance, in those days, from the prison door to the market-place. Measured by the prisoner's experience, however, it might be reckoned a journey of some length; for haughty as her demeanour was, she perchance underwent an agony from every footstep of those that thronged to see her, as if her heart had been flung into the street for them all to spurn and trample upon. In our nature, however, there is a provision, alike marvellous and merciful, that the sufferer should never know the intensity of what he endures by its present torture, but chiefly by the pang that rankles after it. With almost a serene deportment, therefore, Hester Prynne passed through this portion of her ordeal, and came to a sort of scaffold, at the western extremity of the market-place. It stood nearly beneath the eaves of Boston's earliest church, and appeared to be a fixture there.

In fact, this scaffold constituted a portion of a penal machine, which now, for two or three generations past, has been merely historical and traditionary among us, but was held, in the old time, to be as effectual an agent, in the promotion of good citizenship, as ever was the guillotine among the terrorists of France. It was, in short, the platform of the pillory; and above it rose the framework of that instrument of discipline, so fashioned as to confine the human head in its tight grasp, and thus hold it up to the public gaze. The very ideal of ignominy was embodied and made manifest in this contrivance of wood and iron. There can be no outrage, methinks, against our common nature—whatever be the delinquencies of the individual—no outrage more flagrant than to forbid the culprit to hide his face for shame; as it was the essence of this punishment to do. In Hester Prynne's instance, however, as not unfrequently in other cases, her sentence bore that she should stand a certain time upon the platform, but without undergoing that gripe about the neck and confinement of the head, the proneness to which was the most devilish characteristic of this ugly engine. Knowing well her part, she ascended a flight of wooden steps, and was thus displayed to the surrounding multitude, at about the height of a man's shoulders above the street.

Had there been a Papist among the crowd of Puritans, he might have seen in this beautiful woman, so picturesque in her attire and mien, and with the infant at her bosom, an object to remind him of the image of Divine Maternity, which so many illustrious painters have vied with one another to represent; something which should remind him, indeed, but only by contrast, of that sacred image of sinless motherhood, whose infant was to redeem the world. Here, there was the taint of deepest sin in the most sacred quality of human life, working such effect, that the world was only the darker for this woman's beauty, and the more lost for the infant that she had borne.

The scene was not without a mixture of awe, such as must always invest the spectacle of guilt and shame in a fellow-creature, before society shall have grown corrupt enough to smile, instead of shuddering at it. The witnesses of Hester Prynne's disgrace had not yet passed beyond their simplicity. They were stern enough to look upon her death, had that been the sentence, without a murmur at its severity, but had none of the heartlessness of another social state, which would find only a theme for jest in an exhibition like the present. Even had there been a disposition to turn the matter into ridicule, it must have been repressed and overpowered by the solemn presence of men no less dignified than the governor, and several of his counsellors, a judge, a general, and the ministers of the town, all of whom sat or stood in a balcony of the meeting-house, looking down upon the platform. When such personages could constitute a part of the spectacle, without risking the majesty, or reverence of rank and office, it was safely to be inferred that the infliction of a legal sentence would have an earnest and effectual meaning. Accordingly, the crowd was sombre and grave. The unhappy culprit sustained herself as best a woman might, under the heavy weight of a thousand unrelenting eyes, all fastened upon her, and concentrated at her bosom. It was almost intolerable to be borne. Of an impulsive and passionate nature, she had fortified herself to encounter the stings and venomous stabs of public contumely, wreaking itself in every variety of insult; but there was a quality so much more terrible in the solemn mood of the popular mind, that she longed rather to behold all those rigid countenances contorted with scornful merriment, and herself the object. Had a roar of laughter burst from the multitude—each man, each woman, each little shrill-voiced child, contributing their individual parts—Hester Prynne might have repaid them all with a bitter and disdainful smile. But, under the leaden infliction which it was her doom to endure, she felt, at moments, as if she must needs shriek out with the full power of her lungs, and cast herself from the scaffold down upon the ground, or else go mad at once.

Yet there were intervals when the whole scene, in which she was the most conspicuous object, seemed to vanish from her eyes, or, at least, glimmered indistinctly before them, like a mass of imperfectly shaped and spectral images. Her mind, and especially her memory, was preternaturally active, and kept bringing up other scenes than this roughly hewn street of a little town, on the edge of the western wilderness: other faces than were lowering upon her from beneath the brims of those steeple-crowned hats. Reminiscences, the most trifling and immaterial, passages of infancy and school-days, sports, childish quarrels, and the little domestic traits of her maiden years, came swarming back upon her, intermingled with recollections of whatever was gravest in her subsequent life; one picture precisely as vivid as another; as if all were of similar importance, or all alike a play. Possibly, it was an instinctive device of her spirit to relieve itself by the exhibition of these phantasmagoric forms, from the cruel weight and hardness of the reality.

Be that as it might, the scaffold of the pillory was a point of view that revealed to Hester Prynne the entire track along which she had been treading, since her happy infancy. Standing on that miserable eminence, she saw again her native village, in Old England, and her paternal home: a decayed house of grey stone, with a poverty-stricken aspect, but retaining a half obliterated shield of arms over the portal, in token of antique gentility. She saw her father's face, with its bold brow, and reverend white beard that flowed over the old-fashioned Elizabethan ruff; her mother's, too, with the look of heedful and anxious love which it always wore in her remembrance, and which, even since her death, had so often laid the impediment of a gentle remonstrance in her daughter's pathway. She saw her own face, glowing with girlish beauty, and illuminating all the interior of the dusky mirror in which she had been wont to gaze at it. There she beheld another countenance, of a man well stricken in years, a pale, thin, scholar-like visage, with eyes dim and bleared by the lamp-light that had served them to pore over many ponderous books. Yet those same bleared optics had a strange, penetrating power, when it was their owner's purpose to read the human soul. This figure of the study and the cloister, as Hester Prynne's womanly fancy failed not to recall, was slightly deformed, with the left shoulder a trifle higher than the right. Next rose before her in memory's picture-gallery, the intricate and narrow thoroughfares, the tall, grey houses, the huge cathedrals, and the public edifices, ancient in date and quaint in architecture, of a continental city; where new life had awaited her, still in connexion with the misshapen scholar: a new life, but feeding itself on time-worn materials, like a tuft of green moss on a crumbling wall. Lastly, in lieu of these shifting scenes, came back the rude market-place of the Puritan settlement, with all the townspeople assembled, and levelling their stern regards at Hester Prynne—yes, at herself—

who stood on the scaffold of the pillory, an infant on her arm, and the letter A, in scarlet, fantastically embroidered with gold thread, upon her bosom.

Could it be true? She clutched the child so fiercely to her breast that it sent forth a cry; she turned her eyes downward at the scarlet letter, and even touched it with her finger, to assure herself that the infant and the shame were real. Yes these were her realities—all else had vanished!

Sources: Bartleby.com (www.bartleby.com); Nathaniel Hawthorne, *The Scarlet Letter* (Boston: Ticknor, Reed & Fields, 1850).

Holmes, Oliver Wendell

(1809–1894)

Poet, essayist, novelist, lecturer, and physician Oliver Wendell Holmes—like a number of his nineteenth-century American contemporaries—found success in diverse fields of endeavor. As a literary figure, he is best remembered as a member of the Fireside Poets (a popular group of New England verse-makers that also included Henry Wadsworth Longfellow, William Cullen Bryant, John Greenleaf Whittier, and James Russell Lowell) and as the author of the "Breakfast-Table" series of essays, beginning with the collection *The Autocrat of the Breakfast-Table* (1858). In medicine, he is known for establishing the contagious nature of puerperal, or "childbed," fever, a common and deadly disease among pregnant women in his time.

Holmes's life spanned most of the nineteenth century. He was born on August 29, 1809, in Cambridge, Massachusetts, the son of minister and author Abiel Holmes and his second wife, Sarah. A Boston Brahmin (member of the city's wealthy Yankee elite), Holmes was descended on his mother's side from Puritan Massachusetts governor Simon Bradstreet and his wife, the poet Anne Bradstreet. Holmes attended the Philips Academy prep school, graduated from Harvard University in 1829, and began medical studies at Harvard the following year.

By this time, he had already written some 50 poems, including one of his best-known, "Old Ironsides," published in a Boston newspaper in September 1830. "Old Ironsides," which protested a plan to dismantle the eighteenth-century frigate USS *Constitution* for scrap, was reprinted in other newspapers and broadsides around the country. Its popularity triggered a public outcry that saved the famous War of 1812 vessel. Some of Holmes's other well-known poems include "The Chambered Nautilus" (1858) and "The Deacon's Masterpiece; or, The Wonderful One-Hoss Shay" (1858), an attack on Calvinism. Like other members of the Fireside Poets group, Holmes was known for verse that was traditional in form, disciplined in style, and written for popular consumption. Domestic life, contemporary politics, and American legends were frequent themes of this group. Holmes in particular was known for his good humor and faith in progress, earning the moniker "Beacon Street Wit."

After two more years of medical study in Paris, Holmes returned home to complete his thesis and received his medical degree in May 1836. His first collection of verse, simply titled *Poems,* appeared that same year. At around the same time, Holmes began writing essays on medical topics, and three of his prizewinning pieces were published in 1838. In the summer of 1838, he joined the medical faculty at Dartmouth College and became one of the first American instructors to use the microscope in teaching. Known as a gifted instructor, he was appointed professor of anatomy and physiology at Harvard University in 1847.

In June 1840, meanwhile, Holmes married Amelia Lee Jackson, a Boston socialite. Their first son, future U.S. Supreme Court justice Oliver Wendell Holmes, Jr., was born the following year. By this time, Holmes had begun his frequent public lectures, which often attacked medical quackery. In late 1842, he began his research on Boston cases of puerperal fever, concluding that the fever was contagious and commonly spread from one pregnant woman to another by their doctors. His essay on the topic, published in 1843 and reprinted in 1855, met great resistance, and it took years for his conclusion to be accepted by the medical community.

Holmes also had an important association with one of the most significant medical developments of the nineteenth century. In November 1846, he wrote a letter to William T.G. Morton, a Boston dentist who had used ether vapor to relieve pain during an operation at the Massachusetts General Hospital the previous month. Holmes suggested that Morton call the state produced by ether inhalation *anaesthesia,* a word used by the ancient Greeks to mean "without feeling." Within months, ether anesthesia was being used successfully in several countries around the world. The terms "anesthesia" and "anesthetic" became part of common usage.

In the late 1850s, Holmes began publishing a popular series of essays in the new *Atlantic Monthly* magazine. An innovative literary form, these humorous and philosophical musings took a casual, conversation style with dialogue, verse, and fictional settings. Over the course of the next 15 years, Holmes's "Breakfast-Table" pieces were a mainstay of the magazine and appeared in three popular collections: *Autocrat of the Breakfast-Table* (1858), *Professor at the Breakfast-Table* (1860), and *Poet at the Breakfast-Table* (1872).

Holmes published the first of his three novels, *Elsie Venner,* in 1861. The work proved popular despite controversy over its application of scientific ideas to psychological disorders. His subsequent works of long fiction—all of which he referred to as "medicated novels"—were *Guardian Angel* (1867) and *A Mortal Antipathy* (1885).

Holmes became dean of the Harvard Medical School in 1878 and held the post for six years. He resigned from the Harvard faculty in 1882 to devote his full attention to writing. Thereafter, in addition to his last novel, he published two biographies, *John Lothrop Motley* (1876) and *Ralph Waldo Emerson* (1880), and an account of his travels, *Our Hundred Days in Europe* (1887). Holmes died peacefully in his sleep on October 7, 1894, in Cambridge, Massachusetts.

A.J. Wright

See also: Poetry

◇◇
"The Chambered Nautilus," 1857
◇◇

Originally published in the Atlantic Monthly *as part of Holmes's "Breakfast-Table" series, "The Chambered Nautilus" also appeared in the first collection of those magazine pieces,* Autocrat of the Breakfast-Table *(1858). Combining his interests in science and religion, "The Chambered Nautilus" denies the Puritan/Calvinist view of humanity as eternally flawed. Treating the nautilus shell as a metaphor for the human soul—and its example as a "heavenly message"— the poem describes a long, slow process of growth that equates with spiritual evolution, expanding horizons, and, in the end, eternal freedom.*

This is the ship of pearl, which, poets feign,
Sails the unshadowed main,—
The venturous bark that flings
On the sweet summer wind its purpled wings
In gulfs enchanted, where the Siren sings,

And coral reefs lie bare,
Where the cold sea-maids rise to sun their streaming hair.

Its webs of living gauze no more unfurl;
Wrecked is the ship of pearl!
And every chambered cell,
Where its dim dreaming life was wont to dwell,
As the frail tenant shaped his growing shell,
Before thee lies revealed,—
Its irised ceiling rent, its sunless crypt unsealed!

Year after year beheld the silent toil
That spread his lustrous coil;
Still, as the spiral grew,
He left the past year's dwelling for the new,
Stole with soft step its shining archway through,
Built up its idle door,
Stretched in his last-found home, and knew the old no more.

Thanks for the heavenly message brought by thee,
Child of the wandering sea,
Cast from her lap, forlorn!
From thy dead lips a clearer note is born
Than ever Triton blew from wreathèd horn!
While on mine ear it rings,
Through the deep caves of thought I hear a voice that sings:—

Build thee more stately mansions, O my soul,
As the swift seasons roll!
Leave thy low-vaulted past!
Let each new temple, nobler than the last,
Shut thee from heaven with a dome more vast,
Till thou at length art free,
Leaving thine outgrown shell by life's unresting sea!

Sources: Project Gutenberg (www.Gutenberg.org); *The Poetical Works of Oliver Wendell Holmes,* vol. 6 (Boston: Houghton, Mifflin, 1893).

Irving, Washington
(1783–1859)

America's first professional man of letters and international literary celebrity, Washington Irving is best remembered for two immortal short stories—"Rip Van Winkle" and "The Legend of Sleepy Hollow"—both of which appeared in his 1819 collection *The Sketch Book.*

The youngest of 12 children, he was born on April 3, 1783, in New York City. His father, William Irving, had emigrated from Scotland two decades earlier and became a prosperous merchant. His mother, Sarah Sanders Irving, seems to have spoiled her youngest child, perhaps because he was frail and asthmatic.

Washington Irving was an indifferent schoolboy, fond of reading but bored with "that purgatory of boyhood, a schoolroom." What he loved most was exploring the byways of New York, becoming familiar with "every spot where a murder or robbery had been committed, or a ghost seen." Young Irving frequently visited the home of the Paulding family, the in-laws of his oldest brother, William, who lived in Tarrytown, New York, on the Hudson River. There, within a day's travel of the Catskill Mountains, he romped in the woods and developed a lifelong attachment to the region in which many of his most memorable stories are set.

Irving never attended college. Beginning in 1799, he read law off and on, primarily at the office of Josiah Ogden Hoffman, whose two daughters became Irving's close friends. In 1803, he took a long trip with the Hoffmans to Canada, filling notebooks with his impressions of the people and places he encountered. Throughout his life, Irving would use this method to gather material for the stories and essays that poured from his pen.

In 1806, Irving was admitted to the bar "by the grace of God and Josiah Hoffman," who was one of his examiners. He joined his brother John's law office at No. 3 Wall Street in Manhattan but devoted little time to legal practice, instead embarking on a literary career. Had he married Matilda Hoffman, whom he loved deeply, Irving may have followed a more conventional path. After her sudden death in April 1807, however, he abandoned thoughts of matrimony and devoted his full energy and financial resources to travel and writing.

Early Writings

Irving's first literary effort was a series of essays published in his brother Peter's short-lived newspaper, the *Morning Chronicle* (1802–1803), under the pen name "Jonathan Oldstyle, Gent." In these essays, Irving humorously satirized American society and manners, especially the theater of the day. His choice of pseudonym suggests somewhat ambivalent feelings toward the democratic society of Jeffersonian America. As "Jonathan," a common nickname for an American national, Irving clearly identified himself with the young republic; as an "Oldstyle Gentleman," he mocked the barbarity of the masses as well. Thus, Oldstyle complained ruefully that managers failed to keep the playhouse clean and that audiences lacked taste and critical judgment, attending plays only to drink and carouse. At the same time, Jonathan revealed his own vulgarity by ogling fashionable young women in their theater boxes.

Irving displayed his satirical talents again by teaming with his brother William and their friend James K. Paulding to write a series of 20 periodical essays collectively titled *Salmagundi; or, The Whim-Whams and Opinions of Launcelot Langstaff, Esq. and Others* (1807). Imitating the familiar essay form popularized by British writers Joseph Addison and Richard Steele, the young Americans posed as "critics, amateurs, dilettanti, and cognoscenti" who aimed "to instruct the young, reform the old, correct the town, and castigate the age." *Salmagundi* wildly lampooned virtually every aspect of American society, taking swipes at bad actors, pretentious fashions, and Jefferson's red breeches. "If we moralize it shall be but seldom," they promised, "for we are laughing philosophers, and truly of the opinion that wisdom . . . is a plump, jolly dame, who sits in her armchair, laughs right merrily at the farce of life—and takes the world as it comes."

Peak Years

Irving achieved national acclaim with his first book, *Diedrich Knickerbocker's History of New York* (1809), which he originally planned as a parody of Samuel Mitchell's overblown travel guide *The Picture of New York* (1807). Said to be penned by an eccentric antiquarian named Diedrich Knickerbocker, Irving's history irreverently poked fun at New York's colonial past and democratic present. For example, readers learned of how the heroic governor Peter Stuyvesant, in the midst of a duel, fell backward "on his seat of honor" into a velvety soft cushion "which providence . . . or some kindly cow, had benevolently prepared for his reception." In England, *Knickerbocker* delighted such literary giants as Lord Byron and Samuel Taylor Coleridge, while Charles Dickens admitted that he wore out his copy with rereading. Translated into French and German and adapted to the stage, the book established Washington Irving as America's most renowned writer of the day.

Although *Knickerbocker* brought him fame, Irving did not write another book for 10 more years. "I seemed to drift without aim or object," he later recalled. During this period, he became a partner in the family hardware business and moved to Washington, D.C., to lobby against restrictions on trade. He became a popular figure at public functions and was a favorite of first lady Dolley Madison. He also edited a literary journal, *The Analectic Magazine* (1813–1815), but found the routine of editorial work tedious. At length, "weary of everything and myself," Irving set off for Europe in 1815. He hoped to overcome his "idle habits and idle associates" by traveling around the countryside "observing the manners and characters of various parts of it," with the goal of producing a book greater than *Knickerbocker's History.*

After four years in Europe, Irving completed *The Sketch Book of Geoffrey Crayon, Gent.* (1819–1820), generally ranked as his finest work. Originally published as separate magazine pieces and later collected into one volume, *The Sketch Book* combined traveler's tales from England in the voice of an American tourist named Geoffrey Crayon, along with several stories set in America. The two most famous of these stories, "Rip Van Winkle" and "The Legend of Sleepy Hollow," were actually retellings of German folktales, said to have been found in the papers of the late Diedrich Knickerbocker.

As he had so many times before, Irving employed the familiar essay style in this work. Unlike Jonathan Oldstyle or Diedrich Knickerbocker,

In Washington Irving's iconic short story "Rip Van Winkle" (1819), the title character wakes from a 20-year sleep to discover that he has missed the American Revolution.

however, Geoffrey Crayon was an amiable daydreamer who longed to escape "from the commonplace realities of the present" and to take refuge in "the shadowy grandeurs of the past." His sketches of English villagers, taverns, and customs were mild-tempered and appreciative, conjuring a sense of bucolic peacefulness that stood in stark opposition to the industrial capitalism that was transforming both England and America at the time. It was precisely this nostalgic sensibility that captured the hearts of so many readers on both sides of the Atlantic.

Irving spent 17 years in Europe, traveling throughout the British Isles, France, Germany, Austria, and Spain to find new subjects to write about. He was especially productive during his years in Spain (1826–1832), writing a succession of novels, travel books, and serious histories that included *Bracebridge Hall* (1822), *Tales of a Traveller* (1824), *A History of the Life and Voyages of Christopher Columbus* (1828), *A Chronicle of the Conquest of Granada* (1829), *Voyages and Discoveries of the Companions of Columbus* (1831), and *The Alhambra* (1832). All of these works sold well, but none achieved the popularity of his earlier writings.

Returning to the United States in 1832, Irving deliberately turned his attention to American subjects. Later that year, he accompanied U.S. commissioner Henry L. Ellsworth on a tour of the proposed Indian Country in present-day Oklahoma, on which he based the popular *A Tour of the Prairies* (1835). Next, relying on documents borrowed from his friend, the wealthy New York merchant and fur trader John Jacob Astor, Irving produced two histories of the fur trade in the Mountain West: *Astoria* (1836) and *The Adventures of Captain Bonneville* (1837). In these works, Irving attempted to underscore the value of the Far West to the United States and the need to push American claims on the region.

Later Life and Legacy

With the exception of four years as the U.S. minister to Spain (1842–1846), Irving spent the rest of his life at his "Sunnyside" estate near Tarrytown, where he had enjoyed happy times as a boy. During his last years, Irving wrote mostly biographies, producing *Oliver Goldsmith* (1849), *Mahomet and His Successors* (1850), and the five-volume *George Washington* (1855–1860). He completed the last of these shortly before his death, from a heart attack, on November 28, 1859.

Although modern critics generally rank Irving below such contemporaries as Nathaniel Hawthorne and Herman Melville, his writing established a model for those authors and others, as exemplified by Hawthorne's *Mosses from an Old Manse* (1846) and Melville's *Piazza Tales* (1856). Likewise, Irving was among the earliest major literary interpreters of the American West, helping lay a foundation for the likes of Ned Buntline, Bret Harte, and Mark Twain in the decades to come. Above all, Irving signified the maturation of American letters. In 1820, shortly before the appearance of *The Sketch Book,* the Anglican minister Sydney Smith wondered, "And who, the wide world over, reads an American book?" Shortly thereafter, England's greatest writers hailed *The Sketch Book* as a masterpiece. Washington Irving, William Thackeray observed, was "the first ambassador whom the New World of Letters sent to the Old."

James Rohrer

◇◇◇

"Rip Van Winkle" (excerpt), 1819

◇◇◇

*In Washington Irving's classic story "Rip Van Winkle," published with "The
Legend of Sleepy Hollow" and other pieces in* The Sketch Book *(1819), the
title character is a henpecked husband, small-game hunter, and social misfit
in the Catskill Mountains of New York state. Domestic values, civic virtue,
and the hardworking yeoman lifestyle are alien to him. With a sip too many
from his flagon of wine, he escapes into a sleep that lasts 20 years. The story
picks up below as Rip awakes. The landscape has changed, America is an
independent nation, and he personally has escaped the "yoke of matrimony."
Although the charm of the story's hero and the humor of Irving's telling
made "Rip Van Winkle" a popular hit, few readers could have overlooked
its parable about civilization and the passing of the wilderness.*

. . . . On waking, he found himself on the green knoll whence
he had first seen the old man of the glen. He rubbed his eyes—
it was a bright sunny morning. The birds were hopping and
twittering among the bushes, and the eagle was wheeling aloft,
and breasting the pure mountain breeze. "Surely," thought Rip,
"I have not slept here all night." He recalled the occurrences
before he fell asleep. The strange man with a keg of liquor—
the mountain ravine—the wild retreat among the rocks—the
woe-begone party at ninepins—the flagon—"Oh! that flagon!
that wicked flagon!" thought Rip—"what excuse shall I make
to Dame Van Winkle!"

He looked round for his gun, but in place of the clean well-oiled
fowling-piece, he found an old firelock lying by him, the barrel
incrusted with rust, the lock falling off, and the stock worm-eaten.
He now suspected that the grave roysterers of the mountain had
put a trick upon him, and having dosed him with liquor, had
robbed him of his gun. Wolf, too, had disappeared, but he might
have strayed away after a squirrel or partridge. He whistled after
him and shouted his name, but all in vain; the echoes repeated his
whistle and shout, but no dog was to be seen.

He determined to revisit the scene of the last evening's gam-
bol, and if he met with any of the party, to demand his dog and

gun. As he rose to walk, he found himself stiff in the joints, and wanting in his usual activity. "These mountain beds do not agree with me," thought Rip; "and if this frolic should lay me up with a fit of the rheumatism, I shall have a blessed time with Dame Van Winkle." With some difficulty he got down into the glen: he found the gully up which he and his companion had ascended the preceding evening; but to his astonishment a mountain stream was now foaming down it, leaping from rock to rock, and filling the glen with babbling murmurs. He, however, made shift to scramble up its sides, working his toilsome way through thickets of birch, sassafras, and witch-hazel, and sometimes tripped up or entangled by the wild grapevines that twisted their coils or tendrils from tree to tree, and spread a kind of network in his path.

At length he reached to where the ravine had opened through the cliffs to the amphitheatre; but no traces of such opening remained. The rocks presented a high impenetrable wall over which the torrent came tumbling in a sheet of feathery foam, and fell into a broad deep basin, black from the shadows of the surrounding forest. Here, then, poor Rip was brought to a stand. He again called and whistled after his dog; he was only answered by the cawing of a flock of idle crows, sporting high in air about a dry tree that overhung a sunny precipice; and who, secure in their elevation, seemed to look down and scoff at the poor man's perplexities. What was to be done? the morning was passing away, and Rip felt famished for want of his breakfast. He grieved to give up his dog and gun; he dreaded to meet his wife; but it would not do to starve among the mountains. He shook his head, shouldered the rusty firelock, and, with a heart full of trouble and anxiety, turned his steps homeward.

As he approached the village he met a number of people, but none whom he knew, which somewhat surprised him, for he had thought himself acquainted with every one in the country round. Their dress, too, was of a different fashion from that to which he was accustomed. They all stared at him with equal marks of surprise, and whenever they cast their eyes upon him, invariably stroked their chins. The constant recurrence of this gesture induced

Rip, involuntarily, to do the same, when to his astonishment, he found his beard had grown a foot long!

He had now entered the skirts of the village. A troop of strange children ran at his heels, hooting after him, and pointing at his gray beard. The dogs, too, not one of which he recognized for an old acquaintance, barked at him as he passed. The very village was altered; it was larger and more populous. There were rows of houses which he had never seen before, and those which had been his familiar haunts had disappeared. Strange names were over the doors—strange faces at the windows—every thing was strange. His mind now misgave him; he began to doubt whether both he and the world around him were not bewitched. Surely this was his native village, which he had left but the day before. There stood the Kaatskill mountains—there ran the silver Hudson at a distance—there was every hill and dale precisely as it had always been—Rip was sorely perplexed—"That flagon last night," thought he, "has addled my poor head sadly!"

It was with some difficulty that he found the way to his own house, which he approached with silent awe, expecting every moment to hear the shrill voice of Dame Van Winkle. He found the house gone to decay—the roof fallen in, the windows shattered, and the doors off the hinges. A half-starved dog that looked like Wolf was skulking about it. Rip called him by name, but the cur snarled, showed his teeth, and passed on. This was an unkind cut indeed—"My very dog," sighed poor Rip, "has forgotten me!"

He entered the house, which, to tell the truth, Dame Van Winkle had always kept in neat order. It was empty, forlorn, and apparently abandoned. This desolateness overcame all his connubial fears—he called loudly for his wife and children—the lonely chambers rang for a moment with his voice, and then all again was silence.

He now hurried forth, and hastened to his old resort, the village inn—but it too was gone. A large rickety wooden building stood in its place, with great gaping windows, some of them broken and mended with old hats and petticoats, and over the door was painted, "the Union Hotel, by Jonathan Doolittle." Instead of the great tree that used to shelter the quiet little Dutch inn of yore, there now was reared a tall naked pole, with something on the top that looked like a red night-cap, and from it was fluttering a flag, on which was a singular assemblage of stars and stripes—all this was strange and incomprehensible. He recognized on the sign,

His mind now misgave him; he began to doubt whether both he and the world around him were not bewitched.

however, the ruby face of King George, under which he had smoked so many a peaceful pipe; but even this was singularly metamorphosed. The red coat was changed for one of blue and buff, a sword was held in the hand instead of a sceptre, the head was decorated with a cocked hat, and underneath was painted in large characters, GENERAL WASHINGTON.

There was, as usual, a crowd of folk about the door, but none that Rip recollected. The very character of the people seemed changed. There was a busy, bustling, disputatious tone about it, instead of the accustomed phlegm and drowsy tranquillity. He looked in vain for the sage Nicholas Vedder, with his broad face, double chin, and fair long pipe, uttering clouds of tobacco-smoke instead of idle speeches; or Van Bummel, the schoolmaster, doling forth the contents of an ancient newspaper. In place of these, a lean, bilious-looking fellow, with his pockets full of handbills, was haranguing vehemently about rights of citizens—elections— members of congress—liberty—Bunker's Hill—heroes of seventy-six—and other words, which were a perfect Babylonish jargon to the bewildered Van Winkle.

The appearance of Rip, with his long grizzled beard, his rusty fowling-piece, his uncouth dress, and an army of women and children at his heels, soon attracted the attention of the tavern politicians. They crowded round him, eyeing him from head to foot with great curiosity. The orator bustled up to him, and, drawing him partly aside, inquired "on which side he voted?" Rip stared in vacant stupidity. Another short but busy little fellow pulled him by the arm, and, rising on tiptoe, inquired in his ear, "Whether he was Federal or Democrat?" Rip was equally at a loss to comprehend the question; when a knowing, self-important old gentleman, in a sharp cocked hat, made his way through the crowd, putting them to the right and left with his elbows as he passed, and planting himself before Van Winkle, with one arm akimbo, the other resting on his cane, his keen eyes and sharp hat penetrating, as it were, into his very soul, demanded in an austere tone, "what brought him to the election with a gun on his shoulder, and a mob at his heels, and whether he meant to breed a riot in the village?"—"Alas! gentlemen," cried Rip, somewhat dismayed, "I am a poor quiet man, a native of the place, and a loyal subject of the king, God bless him!"

Here a general shout burst from the by-standers—"A tory! a tory! a spy! a refugee! hustle him! away with him!" It was with great difficulty that the self-important man in the cocked hat restored order; and, having assumed a tenfold austerity of brow, demanded again of the unknown culprit, what he came there for, and whom he was seeking? The poor man humbly assured him that he meant no harm, but merely came there in search of some of his neighbors, who used to keep about the tavern.

"Well—who are they?—name them."

Rip bethought himself a moment, and inquired, "Where's Nicholas Vedder?"

There was a silence for a little while, when an old man replied, in a thin piping voice, "Nicholas Vedder! why, he is dead and gone these eighteen years! There was a wooden tombstone in the church-yard that used to tell all about him, but that's rotten and gone too."

"Where's Brom Dutcher?"

"Oh, he went off to the army in the beginning of the war; some say he was killed at the storming of Stony Point—others say he was drowned in a squall at the foot of Antony's Nose. I don't know—he never came back again."

"Where's Van Bummel, the schoolmaster?"

"He went off to the wars too, was a great militia general, and is now in congress."

Rip's heart died away at hearing of these sad changes in his home and friends, and finding himself thus alone in the world. Every answer puzzled him too, by treating of such enormous lapses of time, and of matters which he could not understand: war—congress—Stony Point;—he had no courage to ask after any more friends, but cried out in despair, "Does nobody here know Rip Van Winkle?"

"Oh, Rip Van Winkle!" exclaimed two or three, "Oh, to be sure! that's Rip Van Winkle yonder, leaning against the tree."

Rip looked, and beheld a precise counterpart of himself, as he went up the mountain: apparently as lazy, and certainly as ragged. The poor fellow was now completely confounded. He doubted his own identity, and whether he was himself or another man. In the midst of his bewilderment, the man in the cocked hat demanded who he was, and what was his name?

"God knows," exclaimed he, at his wit's end; "I'm not myself—I'm somebody else—that's me yonder—no—that's somebody else got into my shoes—I was myself last night, but I fell asleep on the mountain, and they've changed my gun, and every thing's changed, and I'm changed, and I can't tell what's my name, or who I am!"

The by-standers began now to look at each other, nod, wink significantly, and tap their fingers against their foreheads. There was a whisper also, about securing the gun, and keeping the old fellow from doing mischief, at the very suggestion of which the self-important man in the cocked hat retired with some precipitation. At this critical moment a fresh comely woman pressed through the throng to get a peep at the gray-bearded man. She had a chubby child in her arms, which, frightened at his looks, began to cry. "Hush, Rip," cried she, "hush, you little fool; the old man won't hurt you." The name of the child, the air of the mother, the tone of her voice, all awakened a train of recollections in his mind. "What is your name, my good woman?" asked he.

"Judith Gardenier."

"And your father's name?"

"Ah, poor man, Rip Van Winkle was his name, but it's twenty years since he went away from home with his gun, and never has been heard of since—his dog came home without him; but whether he shot himself, or was carried away by the Indians, nobody can tell. I was then but a little girl."

Rip had but one question more to ask; but he put it with a faltering voice:

"Where's your mother?"

"Oh, she too had died but a short time since; she broke a blood-vessel in a fit of passion at a New-England peddler."

There was a drop of comfort, at least, in this intelligence. The honest man could contain himself no longer. He caught his daughter and her child in his arms. "I am your father!" cried he— "Young Rip Van Winkle once—old Rip Van Winkle now!—Does nobody know poor Rip Van Winkle?"

All stood amazed, until an old woman, tottering out from among the crowd, put her hand to her brow, and peering under it in his face for a moment, exclaimed, "Sure enough! it is Rip Van Winkle—it is himself! Welcome home again, old neighbor— Why, where have you been these twenty long years?"

Rip's story was soon told, for the whole twenty years had been to him but as one night. The neighbors stared when they heard it; some were seen to wink at each other, and put their tongues in their cheeks: and the self-important man in the cocked hat, who, when the alarm was over, had returned to the field, screwed down the corners of his mouth, and shook his head—upon which there was a general shaking of the head throughout the assemblage.

It was determined, however, to take the opinion of old Peter Vanderdonk, who was seen slowly advancing up the road. He was a descendant of the historian of that name, who wrote one of the earliest accounts of the province. Peter was the most ancient inhabitant of the village, and well versed in all the wonderful events and traditions of the neighborhood. He recollected Rip at once, and corroborated his story in the most satisfactory manner. He assured the company that it was a fact, handed down from his ancestor the historian, that the Kaatskill mountains had always been haunted by strange beings. That it was affirmed that the great Hendrick Hudson, the first discoverer of the river and country, kept a kind of vigil there every twenty years, with his crew of the Half-moon; being permitted in this way to revisit the scenes of his enterprise, and keep a guardian eye upon the river, and the great city called by his name. That his father had once seen them in their old Dutch dresses playing at nine-pins in a hollow of the mountain; and that he himself had heard, one summer afternoon, the sound of their balls, like distant peals of thunder.

To make a long story short, the company broke up, and returned to the more important concerns of the election. Rip's daughter took him home to live with her; she had a snug, well-furnished house, and a stout cheery farmer for a husband, whom Rip recollected for one of the urchins that used to climb upon his back. As to Rip's son and heir, who was the ditto of himself, seen leaning against the tree, he was employed to work on the farm; but evinced an hereditary disposition to attend to anything else but his business.

Rip now resumed his old walks and habits; he soon found many of his former cronies, though all rather the worse for the wear and tear of time; and preferred making friends among the rising generation, with whom he soon grew into great favor.

Having nothing to do at home, and being arrived at that happy age when a man can be idle with impunity, he took his place once more on the bench at the inn door, and was reverenced as one of the patriarchs of the village, and a chronicle of the old times "before the war." It was some time before he could get into the regular track of gossip, or could be made to comprehend the strange events that had taken place during his torpor. How that there had been a revolutionary war—that the country had thrown off the yoke of old England—and that, instead of being a subject of his Majesty George the Third, he was now a free citizen of the United States. Rip, in fact, was no politician; the changes of states and empires made but little impression on him; but there was one species of despotism under which he had long groaned, and that was—petticoat government. Happily that was at an end; he had got his neck out of the yoke of matrimony, and could go in and out whenever he pleased, without dreading the tyranny of Dame Van Winkle. Whenever her name was mentioned, however, he shook his head, shrugged his shoulders, and cast up his eyes; which might pass either for an expression of resignation to his fate, or joy at his deliverance.

He used to tell his story to every stranger that arrived at Mr. Doolittle's hotel. He was observed, at first, to vary on some points every time he told it, which was, doubtless, owing to his having so recently awaked. It at last settled down precisely to the tale I have related, and not a man, woman, or child in the neighborhood, but knew it by heart. Some always pretended to doubt the reality of it, and insisted that Rip had been out of his head, and that this was one point on which he always remained flighty. The old Dutch inhabitants, however, almost universally gave it full credit. Even to this day they never hear a thunderstorm of a summer afternoon about the Kaatskill, but they say Hendrick Hudson and his crew are at their game of nine-pins; and it is a common wish of all hen-pecked husbands in the neighborhood, when life hangs heavy on their hands, that they might have a quieting draught out of Rip Van Winkle's flagon.

Sources: Bartleby.com (www.bartleby.com); Washington Irving, *Rip Van Winkle* and *The Legend of Sleepy Hollow,* vol. X, part 2, Harvard Classics Shelf of Fiction (New York: P.F. Collier & Son, 1917).

Libraries and Lyceums

In British North America and the early United States, literacy and book ownership were signs of status and good breeding. Libraries, therefore, were a long-standing feature of life in the New World, although they remained small and exclusive throughout much of the seventeenth and eighteenth centuries. In the nineteenth century, printed materials became much cheaper and easier to produce and the number and size of libraries grew dramatically, as Americans explored different approaches to collecting and sharing books and periodicals.

Beginning in the early nineteenth century, roughly concurrent with the rise of literary culture and libraries in America, the lyceum— or lecture and discussion hall—emerged as a thriving institution for adult education, public readings, and the airing of social and cultural issues in communities of all sizes. Lecturers on the lyceum circuit—from Ralph Waldo Emerson and Henry David Thoreau to a young Abe Lincoln and the leading voices of the abolitionist and women's rights movements—typically would deliver their lectures on winter evenings at a centrally located building in the community. For many Americans during the antebellum period, the lyceum was a principal means of continuing education and staying abreast of current affairs.

Early American Libraries

The public library as we know it today did not exist at all in colonial America. The largest collections of books, numbering 200–300 volumes, were in the possession of a few wealthy individuals and institutions such as churches and colleges. These early, privately owned libraries were restricted to a handful of individuals, such as family and friends of the owner, parishioners, and students. This was a concern to statesman and printer Benjamin Franklin, who in 1731 persuaded 50 friends to join in founding the Library Company of Philadelphia. Among the first volumes selected by Franklin were an atlas, several dictionaries, and works on philosophy and science. Although this "social library" was restricted to subscribers and did little to encourage the broad spread of knowledge, it served as a model for similar institutions in other cities, including the Redwood Library in Newport, Rhode Island (1747); the Charleston Library Society (1748); and the New York Society Library (1754).

An alternative to the social library emerged in the 1760s. "Circulating" libraries were for-profit concerns, generally owned by a single individual and open to any person who paid a monthly fee. As circulating libraries were dependent on attracting as many subscribers as possible, they generally featured book collections that were large by the day's standards—an average of 3,000 volumes. Their focus tended to skew toward more popular reading materials, such as periodicals and novels, and away from weightier works. Unlike many social libraries, circulating libraries welcomed women as members. Indeed, novels were purchased largely to accommodate their tastes, which were judged to be less serious than those of men.

Libraries in Jacksonian America

In 1820, members of New York's Society for the Prevention of Pauperism proposed the creation of a new type of library geared toward young men, particularly immigrants. Known as "apprentices' libraries," these institutions offered mostly vocational books. The purpose of the apprentices' library was to allow the urban poor to improve themselves and their employment prospects while occupying their time with a wholesome alternative to other pastimes the city offered. Many cities soon followed New York's lead, among them Salem, Massachusetts (1820); Albany, New York (1821); Baltimore, Maryland (1822); Charleston, South Carolina (1824); and Washington, D.C. (1828).

The year 1820 also saw the introduction of another new model: the "mercantile library," first established in Philadelphia. Underwritten by wealthy businessmen, these institutions housed volumes geared toward professionals in the legal and commercial trades. A number of other cities followed Philadelphia's lead in establishing mercantile libraries, while social and professional groups borrowed the idea and established their own specialized institutions. In 1833, for example, African Americans formed the Philadelphia Library Company of Colored Persons, and the Typographical Union in New York established its own library in 1834.

The early decades of the nineteenth century were marked as well by a dramatic expansion in the size and scope of the book collections owned by churches. These libraries, which came to be known as "Sunday school libraries," typically loaned each parishioner one book per week. This was seen as an opportunity to improve both the morals and education of church members, though the collections were geared heavily toward children.

In the 1830s, young Americans also began to benefit from school district libraries. First established in New York in 1838, the idea spread to Massachusetts, where famed educator Horace Mann wrote that libraries were crucial to the development of a "powerful and an exemplary people." By 1850, the state of New York had more than 8,000 school district libraries, with combined holdings in excess of 1 million volumes; Massachusetts had 700 school district libraries. Alabama, Indiana, Michigan, Mississippi, Ohio, and Wisconsin also were quick to embrace the idea.

Antebellum Libraries

The antebellum era witnessed the emergence of two new types of libraries—the two varieties most familiar to Americans today. The first was the research library, a large, scholarly collection of books, generally with access limited to a selected segment of the population. The development of the research library was prompted by a number of trends in American culture. Foremost among these were an increased affinity for science and scholarly analysis, the movement of influential new European schools of thought across the Atlantic, and the proliferation of all manner of scientific and academic periodicals.

The United States' first research library was the Astor Library, established in New York City in 1849 and funded with $400,000 left by business magnate John Jacob Astor in his will. The library, in contrast to most other research collections, was available to anyone who might care to use it, but the materials—scientific works, scholarly periodicals, reference books—were noncirculating and so could be consulted only within the library. Other institutions soon began to follow the lead of the Astor Library, reinventing their collections for more scholarly heft. This included most institutions of higher learning, beginning with Harvard University, which began to invest directly in books rather than simply taking whatever was donated.

Also important was the transformation of the Library of Congress, founded in 1800. Chronically underfunded for its first several decades, the library's collection was made up largely of whatever books could be acquired inexpensively. After a fire destroyed 35,000 of the institution's 50,000 volumes in 1851, Congress appropriated $75,000 for replacements. This level of support continued in subsequent years, allowing the Librarians of Congress to build a world-class research collection. By 1867, it was the largest in the United States—a true "national library."

The other new type of library established in the antebellum era—also starting in 1848—was the public library. In that year, the Massachusetts state legislature passed a bill calling for a library in Boston that would be open to the general public and would be supported at the taxpayers' expense. Prominent scholar George Ticknor took charge of building the Boston Public Library's collection, which numbered 16,000 volumes when it opened for business on May 2, 1854. Two other New England states—Maine and New Hampshire—followed suit in short order, establishing their own public library systems. Elsewhere, however, public libraries did not exist until after the Civil War.

The slow spread of the public library speaks to the controversy that surrounded the idea. Though widely embraced today, public libraries were a hot political issue in the 1850s and 1860s. Some Americans were concerned that the public could not be trusted with the books they borrowed and that volumes would not be returned or would be damaged. Others argued that libraries would become tools of political parties or religious groups, used to inculcate patrons with a particular ideology. Still others simply objected to paying whatever taxes were needed to support public libraries.

Because of these concerns, the public library did not become commonplace in the United States until private individuals and groups began to make a concerted effort to promote and support them after the Civil War. Particularly important in this regard were Ladies' Library Associations, the American Library Association, and steel magnate Andrew Carnegie. Thanks to these efforts, the public library was well established by the start of the twentieth century, having become the most common variety of library to be found in the United States, both then and now.

Lyceums

The founder of the American lyceum movement was Josiah Holbrook, who opened the first such institution—the Society for the Diffusion of Useful Knowledge—in Millbury, Massachusetts, in 1826. The concept soon became popular across New England and, over the course of the next decade, spread to the Upper Atlantic states, the South, and the Midwest. By the mid-1840s, some 4,000 communities across the country had a lyceum for sponsoring public lectures on a host of topics, from the applied sciences to travel, poetry, literary criticism, and philosophy. At first, the lectures were delivered by scholars and other intellectuals. By the 1840s and 1850s, featured speakers included such celebrities as Frederick Douglass, Ralph Waldo Emerson, Wendell Phillips, and Henry David Thoreau.

The relationship between lecturer and audience, according to Holbrook, was critically important to the success of the lyceum. In his view, the lecturer should reach all members of the community, no matter their occupation, social standing, political affiliation, or religious beliefs, and the lecture should be divorced from all partisan ideologies. In reality, lyceum audiences were never as diverse or as apolitical as Holbrook wished. By the mid-1850s, attendees were almost exclusively middle-class, white, Anglo-Saxon, and Protestant. Politicians such as Edward Everett and Daniel Webster sometimes delivered nonsectarian lectures, but they were more renowned for their political talks. Preachers such as Henry Ward Beecher and Theodore Parker delivered lectures on aesthetic topics, but religious messages were never far from their lips. Other lecturers in the 1850s, such as Frederick Douglass, William Lloyd Garrison, and Wendell Phillips, routinely addressed social reform issues, and the abolitionist movement was, according to Emerson, a "fruitful nursery of orators."

Emerson himself was perhaps the most successful and famous lyceum speaker of the antebellum era. Trained for the pulpit as a Unitarian minister, he became a lyceum lecturer in the early 1830s, just as the movement began to seek distinguished lecturers to broaden its programs. Although the programs had usually featured lectures by several prominent speakers, Emerson commanded enough attention to deliver whole series of lectures himself. The lyceum provided him with a platform from which he could elaborate his ideas, develop his literary and oratorical style, and connect with live audiences. He continued this occupation for nearly 50 years, until the end of his life, and managed to make a substantial living from lecturing.

Emerson's chief competitor on the lyceum circuit during the 1840s and 1850s was Frederick Douglass, who began his career as an abolitionist orator in October 1841. Initially, Douglass was employed by the Massachusetts Anti-Slavery Society and the American Anti-Slavery Society, who told him to limit his lectures to a simple narrative of his rise from slavery. But Douglass eventually began to disregard their instructions and to establish himself as an independent and powerful voice on the prevalence of racism in American society and the politics of the antislavery, temperance, and women's rights movements. By the 1850s, he was lecturing throughout the Northern states and as far west as Wisconsin.

The Civil War interrupted the lyceum movement, though it flourished again once the conflict ended. The form and subject matter continued to evolve, incorporating minstrel and vaudeville shows, but the movement provided an audience for many of postbellum America's leading lights, among them Susan B. Anthony, Elizabeth Cady Stanton, Mark Twain, and Victoria Woodhull. In the 1890s, lyceums were finally supplanted by the Chautauqua movement, which offered similar but more diverse programs.

Christopher Bates and James Perrin Warren

See also: Emerson, Ralph Waldo

Longfellow, Henry Wadsworth
(1807–1882)

The most renowned and revered American poet of his time, Henry Wadsworth Longfellow was a man who, according to one critic, if he "had not been born, the time would have created him." Although critics dismissed him as a children's author or an imitative writer of overly sentimental verse, he was widely recognized as America's first non-British writer and honored as the only American to have a bust in Poet's Corner at Westminster Abbey in London. Included in a group of writers dubbed the Fireside Poets (with William Cullen Bryant, Oliver Wendell Holmes, James Russell Lowell, and John Greenleaf Whittier), Longfellow become an icon of the Romantic sentimentality that characterized popular culture in antebellum America and its nostalgia for simpler times, rural family lifestyles, history as legend, and picturesque pastorals.

Early Life and Academic Career

Born on February 27, 1807, in Portland, Maine (then a part of Massachusetts)—far from the artistic and intellectual centers of the new nation—Longfellow grew up in that shipping center with a long family legacy and the pull of the outside world bearing upon his interests. His father was a lawyer; his maternal grandfather was a general in the American Revolution and a founder of Bowdoin College.

At age 15, Longfellow entered Bowdoin, where he began a life-long friendship with Nathaniel Hawthorne. As an undergraduate, Longfellow distinguished himself as both a scholar and a poet, noted for his translations of works by the Roman poet Horace and for publishing a number of his own essays and poems. He idolized Washington Irving and his romanticized sketches of Europe. While a student, Longfellow wrote to his father,

I will not disguise it in the least. . . . [T]he fact is, I most eagerly
aspire after future eminence in literature, my whole soul burns most
ardently after it, and every earthly thought centres in it. . . . I am
almost confident in believing, that if I can ever rise in the world it
must be by the exercise of my talents in the wide field of literature.

After graduating at the age of 18, Longfellow was offered a faculty
position in "modern languages"—the first such position at Bowdoin—
on the condition that he travel to Europe to learn languages and conduct
research for the task. At his father's expense, Longfellow spent three
years in Europe, from 1826 to 1829. Among other experiences, he met
Washington Irving in Spain, who encouraged him in his writing.

Longfellow returned to Maine and, at age 21, assumed his duties as professor and college librarian at Bowdoin. He had learned
French, Italian, Spanish, and some German and immediately set to
work writing textbooks in those languages. He married Mary Storer
Potter of Portland in 1831. In 1833, he published a translation of the
poetry of Spanish poet Jorge Manrique; in 1835, he published a travel
narrative, *Outre-Mer: A Pilgrimage Beyond the Sea.*

Late in 1834, Longfellow was offered a professorship at Harvard
College, on the condition that he spend another year studying
abroad. He and Mary sailed for Europe, where Mary suffered a
miscarriage in October 1835 and died of the effects soon thereafter.
When Longfellow returned home in 1836, he took up his teaching
duties at Harvard and began courting Frances "Fanny" Appleton,
the daughter of one of Boston's wealthy industrialists. After seven
years of persistent courtship, Fanny finally accepted Longfellow's
proposal, and they wed in 1843. Her father bought Craigie House in
Cambridge for them, and Longfellow lived there for the rest of his
life. Fanny eventually bore six children.

Poetry, Fame, and Tragedy

Shortly after the start of his tenure at Harvard, Longfellow began to
publish his poems, along with a few works of prose. Both *Voices of
the Night,* his first collection of poems, and *Hyperion,* a book based on
his travels, appeared in 1839. These were followed by two more collections, *Ballades and Other Poems* (1841) and *Poems on Slavery* (1842),
which *The Dial* called "the thinnest of all of Mr. Longfellow's thin

With such favorites as *The Song of Hiawatha* and "Paul Revere's Ride," Henry Wadsworth Longfellow became the most beloved American poet of the mid-nineteenth century.

books." In 1847, Longfellow published his first famous long poem, the beautifully cadenced *Evangeline: A Tale of Acadie.*

Longfellow retired from the Harvard faculty in 1854 to devote himself full-time to writing. Other significant works of the pre–Civil War period include *Kavanagh: A Tale* (1849), "The Golden Legend" (1851), the famous epic *The Song of Hiawatha* (1855), *The Courtship of Miles Standish* (1858), and "The Children's Hour" (1860). In January 1861, just three months before the outbreak of fighting, he published what would become his best-known poem, "Paul Revere's Ride." Collections of verse include *The Belfry of Bruges and Other Poems* (1845), *The Seaside and the Fireside* (1850), and the much loved *Tales of a Wayside Inn* (1863).

Longfellow enjoyed enormous fame during his lifetime and maintained relationships with many of the leading American writers and thinkers of the time, among them Hawthorne, Lowell, Ralph Waldo Emerson, and Julia Ward Howe. He also visited with and maintained correspondences with friends and admirers abroad, including Thomas Carlyle, Charles Dickens, Fanny Kemble, William Makepeace Thackeray, Anthony Trollope, Alfred Lord Tennyson, Oscar Wilde, Queen Victoria, and Dom Pedro II, the emperor of Brazil. His work was published widely overseas, especially *Hiawatha*, which was translated into 12 languages by the turn of the century.

Personal tragedy struck again in July 1861, when Fanny's cotton muslin dress caught on fire as she was sealing an envelope with hot wax. Longfellow smothered the flames with a rug and his own body, but his wife was badly burned. She died the next day. Longfellow himself was burned so badly that he could not attend her funeral. Burns to his face led him to grow his trademark beard, which he kept for the rest of his life.

Later Years

While he abhorred warfare, as reflected in such poems as "The Arsenal at Springfield" (1848), Longfellow supported the cause of abolition and the Union effort in the Civil War. His two sons joined the Union army and served in combat. After his eldest son, Charles, was wounded in battle in late 1863, Longfellow traveled to Washington to nurse him back to health.

During the years 1864–1867, Longfellow worked on the first English translation of Dante's *Divine Comedy*, assisted in the interpretation and editing by regular meetings at his house of the Dante Club—consisting of James Thomas Fields, William Dean Howells, and Charles Eliot Norton, among others. When he was done with Dante, Longfellow turned to a translation of Michelangelo's poems, though he never completed the work to his satisfaction.

In addition to his scholarly efforts, Longfellow remained active as a poet for the rest of his life. He produced six more collections: *Flower-de-Luce* (1867), *Three Books of Song* (1872), *The Masque of Pandora and Other Poems* (1875), *Kéramos and Other Poems* (1878), *Ultima Thule* (1880), and *In the Harbor* (1882). He also compiled and edited a 31-volume anthology called *Poems of Places*, which brought together verse from around the world.

After a brief illness that proved to be peritonitis, Longfellow died on March 24, 1882. Although he was proclaimed first among American poets at the peak of his career, his reputation went into decline in the decades after his passing, as his writings fell out of step with the twentieth century—the horrors of two world wars, the complexities of Freudian psychoanalysis and existentialism, genocide, and social unrest.

More recent years have brought a reappraisal, as scholars again have come to appreciate Longfellow's contributions to American letters. Besides being a pioneer in the rise of modern literature as a collegiate discipline, he set a new standard for craftsmanship in American poetry and helped encourage worldwide respect for American writers. At the same time, he appropriated materials and forms from other cultures and adapted them to American themes and flavors, and he brought European literature into the American educational curriculum. Longfellow personified a new image of the American scholar as cosmopolitan. Having been educated abroad, he was fluent in French, Italian, and Spanish, and he could read in at least another half-dozen languages. In short, while many scholars may question the quality of his verse, Longfellow's influence unquestionably was extensive and long lasting.

Randal Allred

See also: Poetry

The Song of Hiawatha (excerpt), 1855

Henry Wadsworth Longfellow was antebellum America's most popular poet. The Song of Hiawatha, *an epic poem in 22 chapters, recounts the birth, life, romance, and death of its title character, an Ojibwa Indian prophet. Set on the southern shore of Lake Superior, the poem draws heavily on native legend and folklore. Though not well received by critics, it was an enormous popular success and remains one of the author's best-known works today. The following excerpt tells of Hiawatha's birth and infancy. Wenonah is his mother, Nokomis his grandmother, and Mudjekeewis his spirit-father, the West Wind. As the poem and its popularity suggest, antebellum Americans were fascinated by—and often romanticized—American Indian culture, even if fear and hatred of actual Native Americans was commonplace.*

And the West-Wind came at evening,
Walking lightly o'er the prairie,
Whispering to the leaves and blossoms,

Bending low the flowers and grasses,

Found the beautiful Wenonah,
Lying there among the lilies,
Wooed her with his words of sweetness,
Wooed her with his soft caresses,
Till she bore a son in sorrow,
Bore a son of love and sorrow.

Thus was born my Hiawatha,
Thus was born the child of wonder;
But the daughter of Nokomis,
Hiawatha's gentle mother,
In her anguish died deserted
By the West-Wind, false and faithless,
By the heartless Mudjekeewis.

For her daughter, long and loudly
Wailed and wept the sad Nokomis;
"O that I were dead!" she murmured,
"O that I were dead, as thou art!
No more work, and no more weeping,
Wahonowin! Wahonowin!"

By the shores of Gitche Gumee,
By the shining Big-Sea-Water,
Stood the wigwam of Nokomis,
Daughter of the Moon, Nokomis.
Dark behind it rose the forest,
Rose the black and gloomy pine-trees,
Rose the firs with cones upon them;
Bright before it beat the water,
Beat the clear and sunny water,
Beat the shining Big-Sea-Water.

There the wrinkled old Nokomis
Nursed the little Hiawatha,

Rocked him in his linden cradle,
Bedded soft in moss and rushes,
Safely bound with reindeer sinews;
Stilled his fretful wail by saying,
"Hush! the Naked Bear will hear thee!"
Lulled him into slumber, singing,
"Ewa-yea! my little owlet!
Who is this, that lights the wigwam?
With his great eyes lights the wigwam?
Ewa-yea! my little owlet!"

Many things Nokomis taught him
Of the stars that shine in heaven;
Showed him Ishkoodah, the comet,
Ishkoodah, with fiery tresses;
Showed the Death-Dance of the spirits,
Warriors with their plumes and war-clubs,
Flaring far away to northward
In the frosty nights of Winter;
Showed the broad white road in heaven,
Pathway of the ghosts, the shadows,
Running straight across the heavens,
Crowded with the ghosts, the shadows.

At the door on summer evenings
Sat the little Hiawatha;
Heard the whispering of the pine-trees,
Heard the lapping of the waters,
Sounds of music, words of wonder;
"Minne-wawa!" said the Pine-trees,
"Mudway-aushka!" said the water.

Source: Henry Wadsworth Longfellow, *The Song of Hiawatha* (Leipzig: Alphons Dürr, 1856).

Lowell, James Russell

(1819–1891)

Poet, abolitionist, editor, literary critic, college professor, and diplomat James Russell Lowell was one of nineteenth-century America's most revered men of letters. He is best remembered today as the author of *The Biglow Papers* (1848), one of the first major literary works to employ American vernacular speech. Lowell was associated with the Fireside Poets, a group of popular New England writers in the nineteenth century that also included William Cullen Bryant, Oliver Wendell Holmes, Henry Wadsworth Longfellow, and John Greenleaf Whittier.

Lowell was born on February 22, 1819, in Cambridge, Massachusetts, the youngest and favorite of the five children of Charles and Harriet Lowell. The Lowells were well-respected figures among New England's social and intellectual elite. Charles Lowell, pastor of Boston's West Church until his death in 1861, was the quintessential New England Unitarian minister—genial, rational, optimistic, and moralistic. Harriet was a doting mother who taught her son to read and to sing old English folk ballads. From his parents, James acquired a deep conviction in the importance of ethical behavior and Christian benevolence. From his father, he also inherited a deep hatred of slavery.

Even as a child, Lowell lived in a world of books and learning. A voracious reader, he knew the works of Sir Walter Scott and Edmund Spenser by age 9. From 1827 to 1833, Lowell prepared for college under the tutelage of William Wells, studying Latin, Greek, and mathematics. He passed the Harvard entrance exam in 1834 and enrolled at the university shortly thereafter. Possessing a reservoir of humor and playfulness, Lowell quickly earned a reputation for being wild and impetuous, and he was disciplined repeatedly for violating college rules.

Following his graduation in 1838, Lowell pursued a Harvard law degree, and in 1840, entered into practice. Law held little appeal for Lowell, however, and he soon began to publish his poems and essays in magazines. The year 1841 marked the publication of his first book of verse, *A Year's Life,* which was dedicated to his fiancée, Maria White.

The sister of a Harvard friend, White had met Lowell in December 1839 and married him on December 26, 1844. She was herself an accomplished poet and also deeply committed to the cause of abolitionism. Under her influence, Lowell shifted his focus and energy toward a literary career and antislavery activism. In 1843, he launched a short-lived literary journal, *The Pioneer,* and throughout the 1840s, he composed a stream of poems and essays for various publications, many on abolitionist themes. In 1844, Lowell became a regular editorialist for the *Pennsylvania Freeman;* in 1848, he contributed a weekly column to the *National Anti-Slavery Standard.*

Lowell's best-known contribution to the antislavery movement was *The Biglow Papers,* a satirical masterpiece penned in opposition to the Mexican-American War. Purportedly the collected verse of a Yankee farmer named Hosea Biglow, an impassioned critic of the war and slavery who wrote in the native idiom of the New England countryside, *The Biglow Papers* was alternately ironic, humorous, and acerbic. The work achieved great success in the Northern states and brought Lowell national fame.

Just as Lowell's star began to rise, however, his personal life was marred by tragedy. His daughters Blanche and Rose and his son Walter all died in infancy. Then in 1853, Maria died after a long sickness, leaving the grieving Lowell to raise his daughter Mabel. A nurse named Frances Dunlap was hired to care for the child, and in 1856, Lowell married her. By this time, his grief over Maria's death and his weariness with the constant splits within the antislavery movement had led him to withdraw from active abolitionism.

In 1855, Lowell was invited to deliver a series of lectures on English poetry before Boston's Lowell Institute. The lectures established him as a major literary critic, and he was offered the Smith Professorship of Modern Languages at Harvard College, where he replaced the retiring Henry Wadsworth Longfellow. Over the next 20 years, Lowell produced a steady stream of poetry and literary criticism on writers as diverse as Geoffrey Chaucer, Ralph Waldo Emerson, Jean-Jacques Rousseau, and William Shakespeare. He served as the first editor of *The Atlantic Monthly* (1857–1861) and was a frequent contributor to the *North American Review*. A second series of *Biglow Papers*, dealing with states' rights, the Civil War, and Reconstruction politics, appeared in *The Atlantic Monthly* between January 1862 and May 1866.

After retiring from Harvard, Lowell served as minister to Spain from 1877 to 1880 and as minister to England from 1880 to 1885. While holding these positions, he not only represented American interests abroad but also kept up a demanding schedule of lectures and continued to compose poetry and literary criticism. Following the death of his second wife in 1885, Lowell returned to his home in Massachusetts, where he died on August 12, 1891.

Lowell's fame, which extended to Europe as well as America, rested as much on his literary criticism as on his poetry. While often excluded from the modern curriculum and literary canon, he was considered in his time one of America's greatest poets and scholars. In the stormy decade of the 1840s, few reformers wielded their pen more effectively in the struggle against slavery.

James Rohrer

See also: Poetry

<<<<<<<<<<<<<<<<<<<<<<<<<<<<<<<<<<<<<<<<<<<<<<<<<<<<<

The Biglow Papers, "No. 1" (excerpt), 1848
<<<<<<<<<<<<<<<<<<<<<<<<<<<<<<<<<<<<<<<<<<<<<<<<<<<<<

Regarded as the greatest political satire of nineteenth-century America, James Russell Lowell's Biglow Papers *blends prose and verse in the idiomatic speech of fictional New England farmer Hosea Biglow. The first piece, titled "A Letter from Mr. Ezekiel Biglow of Jaalam to the Hon. Joseph T. Bugkinham, Editor of the Boston Courier, Inclosing a Poem of His Son, Mr. Hosea Biglow," launches a scathing indictment of the Mexican-American War and slavery. At the heart of it lies Biglow's ver-nacular poem, excerpted below. Lowell's satire and use of dialect began a tradition in American letters that continued with the likes of Mark Twain, Ambrose Bierce, H.L. Mencken, and Ring Lardner.*

Ez fer war, I call it murder,—
　　There you hev it plain an' flat;
I don't want to go no furder
　　Than my Testyment fer that;
God hez sed so plump an' fairly,
　　It 's ez long ez it is broad,
An' you 've gut to git up airly
　　Ef you want to take in God.

'Taint your eppyletts an' feathers
　　Make the thing a grain more right;
Taint afollerin' your bell-wethers
　　Will excuse ye in His sight;
Ef you take a sword an' dror it,
　　An' go stick a feller thru,
Guv'ment aint to answer for it,
　　God 'll send the bill to you.

Wut 's the use o' meetin-goin'
　　Every Sabbath, wet or dry,
Ef it 's right to go amowin'
　　Feller-men like oats an' rye?
I dunno but wut it's pooty
　　Trainin' round in bobtail coats,—
But it 's curus Christian dooty
　　This ere cuttin' folks's throats.

They may talk o' Freedom's airy
　　Tell they're pupple in the face,—
It 's a grand gret cemetary
　　Fer the barthrights of our race;
They jest want this Californy
　　So 's to lug new slave-states in
To abuse ye, an' to scorn ye,
　　An' to plunder ye like sin.

Sources: Project Gutenberg (www.gutenberg.org); James Russell Lowell, *The Biglow Papers* (London: Trubner & Co., 1861).

Melville, Herman

(1819–1891)

A towering figure in American literature, best known for his epic novel *Moby-Dick; or, The Whale* (1851), Herman Melville was born in New York City on August 1, 1819. The son of Allan Melvill, an importer and merchant, and Maria Gansevoort, daughter of Battle of Saratoga hero General Peter Gansevoort, he spent his early childhood in relative comfort in New York. When his father's attempt at entering the fur industry failed in 1830, however, the family became destitute, a situation exacerbated by Allan Melvill's sudden death two years later. Maria Melvill moved her children to her brother's farm and, not long thereafter, added an "e" to the family name. Herman Melville was educated at various schools in New York City and upstate New York.

Adventures in the South Pacific

Wanderlust during his early adult years led Melville to take a variety of jobs—as a bank clerk, a bookkeeper, a surveyor on the Erie Canal, and a cabin boy on a ship that traveled to England. Upon his return from London in 1840, Melville worked for a brief time as a teacher. In January 1841, he set sail again, this time heading for the South Seas aboard the whaling ship *Acushnet*. His experiences in the Pacific during the next two years would inspire not only his earliest writings but also *Moby-Dick*.

Upon reaching the Marquesas Islands in July 1842, Melville deserted the *Acushnet* with a shipmate. For nearly a month, Melville lived among the natives, an experience that moved him a few years later to write his first book, *Typee: A Peep at Polynesian Life* (1846) and its sequel, *Omoo* (1847). Although Melville claimed that both works were based in fact, he embellished the story of his stay on the islands so much that the books are now regarded as works of fiction.

After his time living with the natives of the Marquesas, Melville continued to explore the South Pacific, sailing to Tahiti aboard the Australian whaling ship *Lucy Ann*. From there, he sailed to Hawaii on the Nantucket whaling ship *Charles and Henry*. In Honolulu, Melville worked for a time as a clerk and then enlisted in the U.S. Navy. He sailed to Boston aboard the American frigate *United States*, arriving on the Eastern seaboard in October 1844. *Typee* was published to great acclaim less than two years later, and *Omoo* appeared a year thereafter, establishing Melville's early reputation as a writer.

Marriage, Massachusetts, and Moby-Dick

In August 1847, Melville married Elizabeth Shaw, the daughter of Lemuel Shaw, the chief justice of the Massachusetts Supreme Judicial Court. After their wedding, the couple moved to New York City; they would have four children. In the late 1840s and early 1850s, Melville continued to publish fiction. *Mardi*, a sea adventure tale similar to his first two books, was printed in 1849; *Redburn*, a youth story set in the sordid sections of Liverpool, appeared the same year; and *White-Jacket*, a novelization of Melville's time in the U.S. Navy, was released a year later. In 1850, Melville became friends with the writer Nathaniel Hawthorne and purchased a farm near Lenox, Massachusetts, where Hawthorne was then living.

In 1851, Melville published *Moby-Dick*, which he dedicated to Hawthorne. The book tells the story of the whaling ship *Pequod*, commanded by the tenacious Captain Ahab, who leads his crew on a hunt for the great white whale Moby Dick. Today, Melville's novel is widely regarded not only as his greatest work but also as one of the finest American novels ever written. Its dense symbolism, experimental forms, and encyclopedic breadth on whales and the whaling industry have been the subjects of endless academic scholarship.

Yet *Moby-Dick* was not well received in its time. The novel's early readers generally were indifferent, and early reviews did recognize the book's almost mythic scope. A critical piece published in the London *Morning Advertiser* on October 24, 1851, for example, reflected on the impossibility of doing justice to such a mammoth novel. According to the reviewer, *Moby-Dick* exemplified "high philosophy, liberal feeling, abstruse metaphysics properly phrased, soaring speculation," and "a style as many-colored as the theme, yet always good."

Later Career and Death

In 1852, Melville published his first complete failure: *Pierre; or, The Ambiguities*. A difficult novel, dense with exaggerated symbolism and dark philosophical themes similar to those of *Moby-Dick, Pierre* received scathing reviews from American literary critics. A piece published in October 1852 in Philadelphia's *Graham's Magazine*, where Edgar Allan Poe had once worked as an editor, criticized *Pierre* by comparison with both Poe and Hawthorne.

The criticism was devastating to Melville's career. His next two books, *Israel Potter: Fifty Years in Exile* (1855) and *The Piazza Tales* (1856), failed to revitalize the impressive reputation he had earned a decade earlier with the publication of *Typee* and *Omoo. Israel Potter* tells the story of a Revolutionary War veteran who is captured by the British and spends most of the rest of his life trapped in England. Melville wrote the book largely because he needed money; in later years, he essentially disowned it. Among the stories that appear in *The Piazza Tales* are the now respected "Bartleby the Scrivener," about a Wall Street copyist who mysteriously refuses to do his job, as well as the similarly canonical "Benito Cereno," which addressed the issue of slavery. Although *The Piazza Tales* received a measure of praise upon publication, it too was a commercial failure.

Despondent and depressed, with decreased physical and psychological stability, Melville began traveling again with the financial assistance of his father-in-law—first to Europe and the Holy Land, then to visit Hawthorne in Liverpool—before returning to New York in 1857. That year, Melville published his last complete work of long fiction, *The Confidence-Man*. The novel received better reviews than his other recent publications, although contemporary criticism tended to compare it unfavorably against his early work. "*Typee* and *Omoo*," wrote one reviewer, "give us a right to expect something better than any of his later books have been."

In the several years following publication of *The Confidence-Man*, Melville spent his time lecturing about his travels and writings. Eventually, he and his family left Massachusetts to settle permanently in New

Herman Melville's profound symbolic novel *Moby-Dick* (1851) has been adapted to the big screen a number of times, never adequately. Gregory Peck starred as Captain Ahab in a 1956 release.

York City. Melville began writing poetry after the outbreak of the Civil War, publishing a collection of war verse titled *Battle-Pieces and Aspects of the War* in 1866. The response to that volume continued the general trend of distaste for his later work. That same year, Melville secured a position as a deputy inspector of customs at the Port of New York, a post he held until 1885. Dual shadows were cast on this late part of Melville's life by the suicide of his eldest son, Malcolm, in September 1867 and the death of his son Stanwix from tuberculosis in 1886.

In his twilight years, Melville published a few volumes of verse: the epic poem *Clarel* in 1876, *John Marr and Other Sailors* in 1888, and *Timoleon* in 1891. He died at his home in New York City on September 28, 1891, and was buried at Woodlawn Cemetery in the Bronx. At the time of his death, Melville had completed the manuscript for his well-known novella *Billy Budd, Sailor,* but it was not published until 1924. In the author's obituary in the *New York Times,* his successful early work was contrasted with his failed late work. The reporter wrote that Melville "died an absolutely forgotten man." It would take nearly a century for this reputation to be revised and for Melville to assume his place in the pantheon of great American writers.

Corey McEleney

See also: Environment and Nature, Views of; Hawthorne, Nathaniel

◇◇◇

Chapter 42, "The Whiteness of the Whale," *Moby-Dick* (excerpt), 1851

◇◇◇

A masterpiece of antebellum literature, Herman Melville's Moby-Dick; or The Whale *is regarded by many literary critics as the greatest of all American novels, in any era. Narrated chiefly in the voice of an itinerant sailor named Ishmael—but with shifting points of view—the richly symbolic tragedy recounts the voyage of the whaling ship Pequod and the maniacal quest of its captain, Ahab, to exact revenge against the great white whale (Moby Dick) for having taken his leg in a previous encounter. Defying simple description, the novel functions on many levels—at once a gripping adventure tale, social commentary, and work of philosophy about the forces that motivate and destroy men. Although Melville disavowed any express allegorical intention, the book's wealth of symbols, mythical associations, and literary and biblical allusions have invited a host of allegorical interpretations. Not least among these is the view of Ahab as a personification of the antebellum American soul, of the Pequod as a symbol of the American "ship of state," and of their hell-bent mission as a premonition of the Civil War.*

Others have focused on the expressly Shakespearean character of the tragedy and such epic themes as the conflict between free will and fatal-

ism, the illusion of power and the will to destruction, and the inscrutability of good and evil. In Chapter 42, one of the most quoted and analyzed in the book, Ishmael attempts to capture the sublime terror of Moby Dick as symbolized by its defining characteristic—its whiteness. At once empty and opaque, the absence of color and the fullness of light, the whale's whiteness represents the great evil in the world and the unfathomable malice of the Creator, beyond human comprehension. "It was the whiteness of the whale that above all things appalled me," says Ishmael. And it is that feature above all, he concludes, that fired Ahab's obsession.

What the white whale was to Ahab, has been hinted; what, at times, he was to me, as yet remains unsaid.

Aside from those more obvious considerations touching Moby Dick, which could not but occasionally awaken in any man's soul some alarm, there was another thought, or rather vague, nameless horror concerning him, which at times by its intensity completely overpowered all the rest; and yet so mystical and well nigh ineffable was it, that I almost despair of putting it in a comprehensible form. It was the whiteness of the whale that above all things appalled me. But how can I hope to explain myself here; and yet, in some dim, random way, explain myself I must, else all these chapters might be naught.

Though in many natural objects, whiteness refiningly enhances beauty, as if imparting some special virtue of its own, as in marbles, japonicas, and pearls; and though various nations have in some way recognised a certain royal preeminence in this hue; even the barbaric, grand old kings of Pegu placing the title "Lord of the White Elephants" above all their other magniloquent ascriptions of dominion; and the modern kings of Siam unfurling the same snow-white quadruped in the royal standard; and the Hanoverian flag bearing the one figure of a snow-white charger; and the great Austrian Empire, Caesarian, heir to overlording Rome, having for the imperial colour the same imperial hue; and though this pre-eminence in it applies to the human race itself, giving the white man ideal mastership over every dusky tribe; and though, besides, all this, whiteness has been even made significant of gladness, for among the Romans a white stone marked a joyful day; and though in other mortal sympathies and symbolizings, this same hue is made the emblem of many touching, noble things—the innocence of brides, the benignity of age; though among the Red Men of America the giving of the white belt of wampum was the deepest pledge of honour; though in many climes, whiteness typifies the majesty of Justice in the ermine of the Judge, and contributes to the daily state of kings and queens drawn by milk-white steeds; though even in the higher mysteries of the most august religions it has been made the symbol of the divine spotlessness and power; by the Persian fire worshippers, the white forked flame be-

> *It was the whiteness of the whale that above all things appalled me.*

ing held the holiest on the altar; and in the Greek mythologies, Great Jove himself being made incarnate in a snow-white bull; and though to the noble Iroquois, the midwinter sacrifice of the sacred White Dog was by far the holiest festival of their theology, that spotless, faithful creature being held the purest envoy they could send to the Great Spirit with the annual tidings of their own fidelity; and though directly from the Latin word for white, all Christian priests derive the name of one part of their sacred vesture, the alb or tunic, worn beneath the cassock; and though among the holy pomps of the Romish faith, white is specially employed in the celebration of the Passion of our Lord; though in the Vision of St. John, white robes are given to the redeemed, and the four-and-twenty elders stand clothed in white before the great-white throne, and the Holy One that sitteth there white like wool; yet for all these accumulated associations, with whatever is sweet, and honourable, and sublime, there yet lurks an elusive something in the innermost idea of this hue, which strikes more of panic to the soul than that redness which affrights in blood.

This elusive quality it is, which causes the thought of whiteness, when divorced from more kindly associations, and coupled with any object terrible in itself, to heighten that terror to the furthest bounds. Witness the white bear of the poles, and the white shark of the tropics; what but their smooth, flaky whiteness makes them the transcendent horrors they are? That ghastly whiteness it is which imparts such an abhorrent mildness, even more loathsome than terrific, to the dumb gloating of their aspect. So that not the fierce-fanged tiger in his heraldic coat can so stagger courage as the white-shrouded bear or shark.*

Bethink thee of the albatross, whence come those clouds of spiritual wonderment and pale dread, in which that white phantom sails in all imaginations? Not Coleridge first threw that spell; but God's great, unflattering laureate, Nature.†

---

*With reference to the Polar bear, it may possibly be urged by him who would fain go still deeper into this matter, that it is not the whiteness, separately regarded, which heightens the intolerable hideousness of that brute; for, analysed, that heightened hideousness, it might be said, only rises from the circumstance, that the irresponsible ferociousness of the creature stands invested in the fleece of celestial innocence and love; and hence, by bringing together two such opposite emotions in our minds, the Polar bear frightens us with so unnatural a contrast. But even assuming all this to be true; yet, were it not for the whiteness, you would not have that intensified terror.

As for the white shark, the white gliding ghostliness of repose in that creature, when beheld in his ordinary moods, strangely tallies with the same quality in the Polar quadruped. This peculiarity is most vividly hit by the French in the name they bestow upon that fish. The Romish mass for the dead begins with "Requiem eternam" (eternal rest), whence REQUIEM denominating the mass itself, and any other funeral music. Now, in allusion to the white, silent stillness of death in this shark, and the mild deadliness of his habits, the French call him REQUIN.

† I remember the first albatross I ever saw. It was during a prolonged gale, in waters hard upon the Antarctic seas. From my forenoon watch below, I ascended to the overclouded deck; and there, dashed upon the main hatches, I saw a regal, feathery thing of unspotted whiteness, and with a hooked, Roman bill sublime. At intervals, it arched forth its vast archangel wings, as if to embrace some holy ark. Wondrous flutterings and throbbings shook it. Though bodily unharmed, it uttered cries, as some king's ghost in supernatural distress. Through its inexpressible, strange eyes, methought I peeped to secrets which took hold of God. As Abraham before the angels, I bowed myself; the white thing was so white, its wings so wide, and in those for ever exiled waters, I had lost the miserable warping memories of traditions and of towns. Long I gazed at that prodigy of plumage. I cannot tell, can only hint, the things that darted through me then. But at last I awoke; and turning, asked a sailor what bird was this. A goney, he replied. Goney! never had heard that name before; is it conceivable that this glorious thing is utterly unknown to men ashore! never! But some time after, I learned that goney was some seaman's name for albatross. So that by no possibility could Coleridge's wild Rhyme have had aught to do with those mystical impressions which were mine, when I saw that bird upon our deck. For neither had I then read the Rhyme, nor knew the bird to be an albatross. Yet, in saying this, I do but indirectly burnish a little brighter the noble merit of the poem and the poet.

Most famous in our Western annals and Indian traditions is that of the White Steed of the Prairies; a magnificent milk-white charger, large-eyed, small-headed, bluff-chested, and with the dignity of a thousand monarchs in his lofty, over-scorning carriage. He was the elected Xerxes of vast herds of wild horses, whose pastures in those days were only fenced by the Rocky Mountains and the Alleghanies. At their flaming head he westward trooped it like that chosen star which every evening leads on the hosts of light. The flashing cascade of his mane, the curving comet of his tail, invested him with housings more resplendent than gold and silver-beaters could have furnished him. A most imperial and archangelical apparition of that unfallen, western world, which to the eyes of the old trappers and hunters revived the glories of those primeval times when Adam walked majestic as a god, bluff-browed and fearless as this mighty steed. Whether marching amid his aides and marshals in the van of countless cohorts that endlessly streamed it over the plains, like an Ohio; or whether with his circumambient subjects browsing all around at the horizon, the White Steed gallopingly reviewed them with warm nostrils reddening through his cool milkiness; in whatever aspect he presented himself, always to the bravest Indians he was the object of trembling reverence and awe. Nor can it be questioned from what stands on legendary record of this noble horse, that it was his spiritual whiteness chiefly, which so clothed him with divineness; and that this divineness had that in it which, though commanding worship, at the same time enforced a certain nameless terror.

I assert, then, that in the wondrous bodily whiteness of the bird chiefly lurks the secret of the spell; a truth the more evinced in this, that by a solecism of terms there are birds called grey albatrosses; and these I have frequently seen, but never with such emotions as when I beheld the Antarctic fowl.

But how had the mystic thing been caught? Whisper it not, and I will tell; with a treacherous hook and line, as the fowl floated on the sea. At last the Captain made a postman of it; tying a lettered, leathern tally round its neck, with the ship's time and place; and then letting it escape. But I doubt not, that leathern tally, meant for man, was taken off in Heaven, when the white fowl flew to join the wing-folding, the invoking, and adoring cherubim!

But there are other instances where this whiteness loses all that accessory and strange glory which invests it in the White Steed and Albatross.

What is it that in the Albino man so peculiarly repels and often shocks the eye, as that sometimes he is loathed by his own kith and kin! It is that whiteness which invests him, a thing expressed by the name he bears. The Albino is as well made as other men—has no substantive deformity—and yet this mere aspect of all-pervading whiteness makes him more strangely hideous than the ugliest abortion. Why should this be so?

Nor, in quite other aspects, does Nature in her least palpable but not the less malicious agencies, fail to enlist among her forces this crowning attribute of the terrible. From its snowy aspect, the gauntleted ghost of the Southern Seas has been denominated the White Squall. Nor, in some historic instances, has the art of human malice omitted so potent an auxiliary. How wildly it heightens the effect of that passage in Froissart, when, masked in the snowy symbol of their faction, the desperate White Hoods of Ghent murder their bailiff in the market-place!

Nor, in some things, does the common, hereditary experience of all mankind fail to bear witness to the supernaturalism of this hue. It cannot well be doubted, that the one visible quality in the aspect of the dead which most appals the gazer, is the marble pallor lingering there; as if indeed that pallor were as much like the badge of consternation in the other world, as of mortal trepidation here. And from that pallor of the dead, we borrow the expressive hue of the shroud in which we wrap them. Nor even in our superstitions do we fail to throw the same snowy mantle round our phantoms; all ghosts rising in a milk-white fog—Yea, while these terrors seize us, let us add, that even the king of terrors, when personified by the evangelist, rides on his pallid horse.

Therefore, in his other moods, symbolize whatever grand or gracious thing he will by whiteness, no man can deny that in its profoundest idealized significance it calls up a peculiar apparition to the soul.

But though without dissent this point be fixed, how is mortal man to account for it? To analyse it, would seem impossible. Can we, then, by the citation of some of those instances wherein this thing of whiteness—though for the time either wholly or in great part stripped of all direct associations calculated to impart to it aught fearful, but nevertheless, is found to exert over us the same sorcery, however modified;—can we thus hope to light upon some chance clue to conduct us to the hidden cause we seek?

Let us try. But in a matter like this, subtlety appeals to subtlety, and without imagination no man can follow another into these halls. And though, doubtless, some at least of the imaginative impressions about to be presented may have been shared by most men, yet few perhaps were entirely conscious of them at the time, and therefore may not be able to recall them now.

Why to the man of untutored ideality, who happens to be but loosely acquainted with the peculiar character of the day, does the bare mention of Whitsuntide marshal in the fancy such long, dreary, speechless processions of slow-pacing pilgrims, down-cast and hooded with new-fallen snow? Or, to the unread, unsophisticated Protestant of the Middle American States, why does the passing mention of a White Friar or a White Nun, evoke such an eyeless statue in the soul?

Or what is there apart from the traditions of dungeoned warriors and kings (which will not wholly account for it) that makes the White Tower of London tell so much more strongly on the imagination of an untravelled American, than those other storied structures, its neighbors—the Byward Tower, or even the Bloody? And those sublimer towers, the White Mountains of New Hampshire, whence, in peculiar moods, comes that gigantic ghostliness over the soul at the bare mention of that name, while the thought of Virginia's Blue Ridge is full of a soft, dewy, distant dreaminess? Or why, irrespective of all latitudes and longitudes, does the name of the White Sea exert such a spectralness over the fancy, while that of the Yellow Sea lulls us with mortal thoughts of long lacquered mild afternoons on the waves, followed by the gaudiest and yet sleepiest of sunsets? Or, to choose a wholly unsubstantial instance, purely addressed to the fancy, why, in reading the old fairy tales of Central Europe, does "the tall pale man" of the Hartz forests, whose changeless pallor unrustlingly glides through the green of the groves—why is this phantom more terrible than all the whooping imps of the Blocksburg?

Nor is it, altogether, the remembrance of her cathedral-toppling earthquakes; nor the stampedoes of her frantic seas; nor the tearlessness of arid skies that never rain; nor the sight of her wide field of leaning spires, wrenched cope-stones, and crosses all adroop (like canted yards of anchored fleets); and her suburban avenues of house-walls lying over upon each other, as a tossed pack of cards;—it is not these things alone which make tearless Lima, the strangest, saddest city thou can'st see. For Lima has taken the white veil; and there is a higher horror in this whiteness of her woe. Old as Pizarro, this whiteness keeps her ruins for ever new; admits not the cheerful greenness of complete decay; spreads over her broken ramparts the rigid pallor of an apoplexy that fixes its own distortions.

I know that, to the common apprehension, this phenomenon of whiteness is not confessed to be the prime agent in exaggerating the terror of objects otherwise terrible; nor to the unimaginative mind is there aught of terror in those appearances whose awfulness to another mind almost solely consists in this one phenomenon, especially when exhibited under any form at all approaching to muteness or universality. What I mean by these two statements may perhaps be respectively elucidated by the following examples.

First: The mariner, when drawing nigh the coasts of foreign lands, if by night he hear the roar of breakers, starts to vigilance, and feels just enough of trepidation to sharpen all his faculties; but under precisely similar circumstances, let him be called from his hammock to view his ship sailing through a midnight sea of milky whiteness—as if from encircling headlands shoals of combed white bears were swimming round him, then he feels a silent, superstitious dread; the shrouded phantom of the whitened waters is horrible to him as a real ghost; in vain the lead assures him he is still off soundings; heart and helm they both go down; he never rests till blue water is under him again. Yet where is the mariner who will tell thee, "Sir, it was not so much the fear of striking hidden rocks, as the fear of that hideous whiteness that so stirred me?"

Second: To the native Indian of Peru, the continual sight of the snowhowdahed Andes conveys naught of dread, except, perhaps, in the mere fancying of the eternal frosted desolateness reigning at such vast altitudes, and the natural conceit of what a fearfulness it would be to lose oneself in such inhuman solitudes. Much the same is it with the backwoodsman of the West, who with comparative indifference views an unbounded prairie sheeted with driven snow, no shadow of tree or twig to break the fixed trance of whiteness. Not so the sailor, beholding the scenery of the Antarctic seas; where at times, by some infernal trick of legerdemain in the powers of frost and air, he, shivering and half shipwrecked, instead of rainbows speaking hope and solace to his misery, views what seems a boundless churchyard grinning upon him with its lean ice monuments and splintered crosses.

But thou sayest, methinks that white-lead chapter about whiteness is but a white flag hung out from a craven soul; thou surrenderest to a hypo, Ishmael.

Tell me, why this strong young colt, foaled in some peaceful valley of Vermont, far removed from all beasts of prey—why is it that upon the sunniest day, if you but shake a fresh buffalo robe behind him, so that he cannot even see it, but only smells its wild animal muskiness—why will he start, snort, and with bursting eyes paw the ground in phrensies of affright? There is no remembrance in him of any gorings of wild creatures in his green northern home, so that the strange muskiness he smells cannot recall to him anything associated with the experience of former perils; for what knows he, this New England colt, of the black bisons of distant Oregon?

No; but here thou beholdest even in a dumb brute, the instinct of the knowledge of the demonism in the world. Though thousands of miles from Oregon, still when he smells that savage musk, the rending, goring bison herds are as present as to the deserted wild foal of the prairies, which this instant they may be trampling into dust.

Thus, then, the muf-
fled rollings of a milky
sea; the bleak rustlings
of the festooned frosts
of mountains; the deso-

> *Though in many of its aspects this visible world seems formed in love, the invisible spheres were formed in fright.*

late shiftings of the windrowed snows of prairies; all these, to Ishmael, are as the shaking of that buffalo robe to the fright-ened colt!

Though neither knows where lie the nameless things of which the mystic sign gives forth such hints; yet with me, as with the colt, somewhere those things must exist. Though in many of its aspects this visible world seems formed in love, the invisible spheres were formed in fright.

But not yet have we solved the incantation of this whiteness, and learned why it appeals with such power to the soul; and more strange and far more portentous—why, as we have seen, it is at once the most meaning symbol of spiritual things, nay, the very veil of the Christian's Deity; and yet should be as it is, the intensifying agent in things the most appalling to mankind.

Is it that by its indefiniteness it shadows forth the heartless voids and immensities of the universe, and thus stabs us from behind with the thought of annihilation, when beholding the white depths of the milky way? Or is it, that as in essence white-ness is not so much a colour as the visible absence of colour; and at the same time the concrete of all colours; is it for these reasons that there is such a dumb blankness, full of meaning, in a wide landscape of snows—a colourless, all-colour of atheism from which we shrink? And when we consider that other theory of the natural philosophers, that all other earthly hues—every stately or lovely emblazoning—the sweet tinges of sunset skies and woods; yea, and the gilded velvets of butterflies, and the but-terfly cheeks of young girls; all these are but subtile deceits, not actually inherent in substances, but only laid on from without; so that all deified Nature absolutely paints like the harlot, whose allurements cover nothing but the charnel-house within; and when we proceed further, and consider that the mystical cosmetic which produces every one of her hues, the great principle of light, for ever remains white or colourless in itself, and if operating without medium upon matter, would touch all objects, even tulips and roses, with its own blank tinge—pondering all this, the palsied universe lies before us a leper; and like wilful travellers in Lapland, who refuse to wear coloured and colouring glasses upon their eyes, so the wretched infidel gazes himself blind at the monumental white shroud that wraps all the prospect around him. And of all these things the Albino whale was the symbol. Wonder ye then at the fiery hunt?

Source: Herman Melville, *Moby-Dick* (Boston: C.H. Simonds, 1926).

Poe, Edgar Allan

(1809–1849)

———— ᛤ ————

Famous for his macabre, psychologically thrilling short stories and musical poetry, his inconstant lifestyle, and his mysterious death, Edgar Allan Poe was one of antebellum America's most innovative and colorful literary figures. Since his passing, he has exerted a substantial influence on other writers and poets, both in the United States and abroad.

In literary circles, Poe was known for his critical reviews and keen eye for talent. His collected reviews, *The Literati of New York* (1846), promoted the careers of such early-nineteenth-century American writers as Nathaniel Hawthorne, Caroline Kirkland, and Epes Sargent. His critical theory, formulated in *The Poetic Principle* (1848), foreshadowed the rules and methods of New Criticism, the leading literary theory of modernism.

Early Years

Poe was born on January 19, 1809, in Boston, Massachusetts. His parents, David Poe and Elizabeth Arnold, were traveling actors, and his father abandoned the family during Poe's infancy. The boy's mother died of tuberculosis a month before his third birthday; he lived with several foster parents before being taken in as the ward of Richmond, Virginia, merchant John Allan. Poe spent his early childhood in London with the Allan family before they returned to Richmond in 1820; the Allans never formally adopted the future author.

Upon receiving an inheritance from his friend William Galt, John Allan amassed a sizable fortune and supported his foster son's education at the University of Virginia, where Poe enrolled in 1826. The young man's substantial gambling debts led to a rift between him and Allan, however, and Poe moved to Boston the following year.

In 1827, while supporting himself in Boston as a newspaper reporter, Poe anonymously published his first book of verse, *Tamerlane and Other Poems.* That same year, at the age of 18, he enlisted in the U.S. Army under the assumed name Edgar A. Perry. His military career began with a posting at Fort Independence in Boston Harbor, after which he was transferred to Fort Moultrie in South Carolina. Two years later, Poe received an early discharge and reconciled with Allan, who helped secure him an appointment to the U.S. Military Academy at West Point. Before entering West Point, Poe published his second collection of verse, *Al Aaraaf, Tamerlane, and Minor Poems* (1829). He also moved to Baltimore to live with his aunt Maria Clemm and his first cousin Virginia, who would one day become Poe's wife.

Poe's career at the U.S. Military Academy proved to be short-lived. He was unhappy and ceased attending classes and church services. In January 1831, less than a year after taking the academy's oath, he appeared for a dress parade wearing gloves and nothing else. This was the last straw, and Poe got his wish—dismissal. In the months that followed, he traveled to New York and published his third volume of poetry, *Poems by Edgar A. Poe* (1831), which he dedicated to "the U.S. Corps of Cadets."

Literary Celebrity

Even after the publication of his third book of poems, Poe continued his wanderlust ways, returning to Baltimore once again to live with his aunt and cousin. It was during this time that his literary ambitions moved beyond poetry, as he began publishing prose in a variety of literary magazines and journals. In 1833, Poe attracted attention when his short story "Ms. Found in a Bottle" won a competition sponsored by the *Baltimore Saturday Visiter.* With the help of an affluent Baltimore resident, Poe landed an assistant editor's position at the *Southern Literary Messenger,* to which he contributed fiction, reviews, and poems. The job did not last long, however, as a salary dispute and a worsening drinking problem led to Poe's dismissal.

On September 22, 1835, Poe married his cousin Virginia Clemm, then only 13 years old, in a secret ceremony; after Virginia turned 14, the couple married publicly. In February 1837, Poe moved to New York with his wife and her mother. A year later, he published his only complete novel, *The Narrative of Arthur Gordon Pym.*

Short-story writer and poet Edgar Allan Poe was a master of the Gothic macabre and a pioneer of detective fiction.

Although Poe's literary celebrity did not develop until the mid-1840s, *The Narrative of Arthur Gordon Pym* displays many of the trademarks for which Poe would become famous. Writing more than a century later in 1950, the poet W.H. Auden praised Poe's novel for its breadth of "adventure," including "shipwreck," "mutiny," "strange natives," and "supernatural nightmare events." In Poe's time, however, the novel was only a marginal success. By 1839, a year after its publication, only 100 copies had been sold in the United States.

Despite the sluggish sales of his novel, Poe's career continued to blossom. From 1839 to 1840, after moving to Philadelphia, he served as coeditor of *Burton's Gentleman's Magazine,* to which he contributed a number of creative and critical pieces. In 1840, a Philadelphia publisher printed Poe's first collection of short stories, *Tales of the Grotesque and Arabesque.* Greeted by mixed reviews, the two-volume edition included the chilling short story "The Fall of the House of Usher." Incorporating the standard conventions of European Gothic fiction—a spooky house, a vault, a storm, a romance novel within the story, hysterical and mad characters, and a general tone of fear—"The Fall of the House of Usher" helped establish the genre that would become the American horror novel, influencing such twentieth-century writers as Ray Bradbury, H.P. Lovecraft, and Stephen King.

From *Burton's*, Poe moved on to a position as literary editor at *Graham's Magazine*, in which he published his stories "The Murders in the Rue Morgue," "The Oval Portrait," and "The Masque of Red Death." In 1842, he published *The Gift: A Christmas and New Year's Present for 1843*, which included the famous tale "The Pit and the Pendulum." That same year, Virginia began manifesting signs of tuberculosis, and the stress led Poe to drink heavily.

Concurrent with Poe's mental decline was a rise in his literary celebrity. In 1843, he was invited by James Russell Lowell to contribute to the magazine *The Pioneer*. In addition to his popular poem "Lenore," Poe submitted what would become one of his most famous short stories, "The Tell-Tale Heart." That same year, he won a prize for his story "The Gold-Bug" and went on a lecture tour titled "Poets and Poetry of America." Moving back to New York in 1844, he went to work for *The Evening Mirror*, where he published "The Raven," the poem that would secure his status as one of the most famous writers in American history.

Delirium and Death

By the time of Virginia's death in New York in 1847, Poe had begun to manifest signs of severe depression. For the next two years, he moved around various cities in the Northeast, continuing to publish and lecture on poetry.

In the fall of 1849, on his way to Philadelphia or New York on business, Poe stopped in Baltimore. On October 3, he was found lying outside a saloon—delirious, in distress, and wearing someone else's clothes. He was immediately taken to a hospital but, after several days of tremors and hallucinations, entered into a coma and died on October 7. Because no autopsy was performed, the cause of death, reported in newspapers as "congestion of the brain," remains shrouded in mystery. It has been attributed, at various times, to suicide, drug overdose, alcoholism, cholera, encephalitis, heart disease, rabies, and a host of other causes. Poe was interred at Westminster Burial Ground in Baltimore.

Influence

In the century and a half since his death, Edgar Allan Poe's influence on American, European, and world literature has been extensive. To begin with, the general themes, forms, and tones of his work have had a profound influence on the horror genre of popular literature. Additionally, Poe's trilogy of famous stories about Detective C. Auguste Dupin—"The Murders in the Rue Morgue" (1841), "The Mystery of Marie Roget" (1842), and "The Purloined Letter" (1844)—is generally regarded by literary scholars as the genesis of the detective fiction and mystery genres.

Because Poe's work tended to straddle the divide between high and low art, the influence of his poetry and fiction can be seen not only in the writings of such canonical American authors as Herman Melville, Walt Whitman, and William Faulkner, but also in theater, film, and even television. His dark strain of Romanticism was particularly influential in France, where it was translated and admired by the Symbolist poets Charles Baudelaire and Stéphane Mallarmé.

Corey McEleney

See also: Poetry

"The Tell-Tale Heart," 1843

Gothic fiction was one of the most popular genres of literature in the early republic, and its most skilled practitioner was the troubled and mercurial author and poet Edgar Allan Poe. His story "The Tell-Tale Heart," first published in James Russell Lowell's journal The Pioneer *in January 1843, is among his best-known works and still is widely read today. A sparsely told tale—we never learn the narrator's name or gender or his or her relationship to the deceased—it remains as chilling as any modern-day horror story. Among Victorian Gothic authors, Poe is known for his focus on the psychology of madness. Readers of "The Tell-Tale Heart" may pause to wonder: Whose heart does the narrator actually hear?*

True!—nervous—very, very dreadfully nervous I had been and am; but why will you say that I am mad? The disease had sharpened my senses—not destroyed—not dulled them. Above all was the sense of hearing acute. I heard all things in the heaven and in the earth. I heard many things in hell. How, then, am I mad? Hearken! and observe how healthily—how calmly I can tell you the whole story.

It is impossible to say how first the idea entered my brain; but once conceived, it haunted me day and night. Object there was none. Passion there was none. I loved the old man. He had never wronged me. He had never given me insult. For his gold I had no desire. I think it was his eye! yes, it was this! He had the eye of a vulture—a pale blue eye, with a film over it. Whenever it fell upon me, my blood ran cold; and so by degrees—very gradually—I made up my mind to take the life of the old man, and thus rid myself of the eye forever.

Now this is the point. You fancy me mad. Madmen know nothing. But you should have seen me. You should have seen how wisely I proceeded—with what caution—with what foresight—with what dissimulation I went to work! I was never kinder to the old man than during the whole week before I killed him. And every night, about midnight, I turned the latch of his door and opened it—oh so gently! And then, when I had made an opening sufficient for my head, I put in a dark lantern, all closed, closed, that no light shone out, and then I thrust in my head. Oh, you would have laughed to see how cunningly I thrust it in! I moved it slowly—very, very slowly, so that I might not disturb the old man's sleep. It took me an hour to place my whole head within the opening so far that I could see him as he lay upon his bed. Ha! would a madman have been so wise as this, And then, when my head was well in the room, I undid the lantern cautiously-oh, so cautiously—cautiously (for the hinges creaked)—I undid it just so much that a single thin ray fell upon the vulture eye. And this I did for seven long nights—every night just at midnight—but I found the eye always closed; and so it

[I]t was not the old man who vexed me, but his Evil Eye.

was impossible to do the work; for it was not the old man who vexed me, but his Evil Eye. And every morning, when the day broke, I went boldly into the chamber, and spoke courageously to him, calling him by name in a hearty tone, and inquiring how he has passed the night. So you see he would have been a very profound old man, indeed, to suspect that every night, just at twelve, I looked in upon him while he slept.

Upon the eighth night I was more than usually cautious in opening the door. A watch's minute hand moves more quickly than did mine. Never before that night had I felt the extent of my own powers—of my sagacity. I could scarcely contain my feelings of triumph. To think that there I was, opening the door, little by little, and he not even to dream of my secret deeds or thoughts. I fairly chuckled at the idea; and perhaps he heard me; for he moved on the bed suddenly, as if startled. Now you may think that I drew back—but no. His room was as black as pitch with the thick darkness, (for the shutters were close fastened, through fear of robbers,) and so I knew that he could not see the opening of the door, and I kept pushing it on steadily, steadily.

I had my head in, and was about to open the lantern, when my thumb slipped upon the tin fastening, and the old man sprang up in bed, crying out—"Who's there?"

I kept quite still and said nothing. For a whole hour I did not move a muscle, and in the meantime I did not hear him lie down. He was still sitting up in the bed listening;—just as I have done, night after night, hearkening to the death watches in the wall.

Presently I heard a slight groan, and I knew it was the groan of mortal terror. It was not a groan of pain or of grief—oh, no!—it was the low stifled sound that arises from the bottom of the soul when overcharged with awe. I knew the sound well. Many a night, just at midnight, when all the world slept, it has welled up from my own bosom, deepening, with its dreadful echo, the terrors that distracted me. I say I knew it well. I knew what the old man felt, and pitied him, although I chuckled at heart. I knew that he had been lying awake ever since the first slight noise, when he had turned in the bed. His fears had been ever since growing upon him. He had been trying to fancy them causeless, but could not.

He had been saying to himself—"It is nothing but the wind in the chimney—it is only a mouse crossing the floor," or "It is merely a cricket which has made a single chirp." Yes, he had been trying to comfort himself with these suppositions: but he had found all in vain. All in vain; because Death, in approaching him had stalked with his black shadow before him, and enveloped the victim. And it was the mournful influence of the unperceived shadow that caused him to feel—although he neither saw nor heard—to feel the presence of my head within the room.

When I had waited a long time, very patiently, without hearing him lie down, I resolved to open a little—a very, very little crevice in the lantern. So I opened it—you cannot imagine how stealthily, stealthily—until, at length a simple dim ray, like the thread of the spider, shot from out the crevice and fell full upon the vulture eye.

It was open—wide, wide open—and I grew furious as I gazed upon it. I saw it with perfect distinctness—all a dull blue, with a hideous veil over it that chilled the very marrow in my bones; but I could see nothing else of the old man's face or person: for I had directed the ray as if by instinct, precisely upon the damned spot.

And have I not told you that what you mistake for madness is but over-acuteness of the sense?—now, I say, there came to my ears a low, dull, quick sound, such as a watch makes when enveloped in cotton. I knew that sound well, too. It was the beating of the old man's heart. It increased my fury, as the beating of a drum stimulates the soldier into courage.

But even yet I refrained and kept still. I scarcely breathed. I held the lantern motionless. I tried how steadily I could maintain the ray upon the eve. Meantime the hellish tattoo of the heart increased. It grew quicker and quicker, and louder and louder every instant. The old man's terror must have been extreme! It grew louder, I say, louder every moment!—do you mark me well I have told you that I am nervous: so I am. And now at the dead hour of the night, amid the dreadful silence of that old house, so strange a noise as this excited me to uncontrollable terror. Yet, for some minutes longer I refrained and stood still. But the beating grew louder, louder! I thought the heart must burst. And now a new anxiety seized me—the sound would be heard by a neighbour! The old man's hour had come! With a loud yell, I threw open the lantern and leaped into the room. He shrieked once—once only. In an instant I dragged him to the floor, and pulled the heavy bed over him. I then smiled gaily, to find the deed so far done. But, for many minutes, the heart beat on with a muffled sound. This, however, did not vex me; it would not be heard through the wall. At length it ceased. The old man was dead. I removed the bed and examined the corpse. Yes, he was stone, stone dead. I placed my hand upon the heart and held it there many minutes. There was no pulsation. He was stone dead. His eye would trouble me no more.

If still you think me mad, you will think so no longer when I describe the wise precautions I took for the concealment of the body. The night waned, and I worked hastily, but in silence. First of all I dismembered the corpse. I cut off the head and the arms and the legs.

I then took up three planks from the flooring of the chamber, and deposited all between the scantlings. I then replaced the boards so cleverly, so cunningly, that no human eye—not even his—could have detected any thing wrong. There was nothing to wash out—no stain of any kind—no blood-spot whatever. I had been too wary for that. A tub had caught all—ha! ha!

When I had made an end of these labors, it was four o'clock—still dark as midnight. As the bell sounded the hour, there came a knocking at the street door. I went down to open it with a light heart,—for what had I now to fear? There entered three men, who introduced themselves, with perfect suavity, as officers of the police. A shriek had been heard by a neighbour during the night; suspicion of foul play had been aroused; information had been lodged at the police office, and they (the officers) had been deputed to search the premises.

I smiled,—for what had I to fear? I bade the gentlemen welcome. The shriek, I said, was my own in a dream. The old man, I mentioned, was absent in the country. I took my visitors all over the house. I bade them search—search well. I led them, at length, to his chamber. I showed them his treasures, secure, undisturbed. In the enthusiasm of my confidence, I brought chairs into the room, and desired them here to rest from their fatigues, while I myself, in the wild audacity of my perfect triumph, placed my own seat upon the very spot beneath which reposed the corpse of the victim.

The officers were satisfied. My manner had convinced them. I was singularly at ease. They sat, and while I answered cheerily, they chatted of familiar things. But, ere long, I felt myself getting pale and wished them gone. My head ached, and I fancied a ringing in my ears: but still they sat and still chatted. The ringing became more distinct:—It continued and became more distinct: I talked more freely to get rid of the feeling: but it continued and gained definiteness—until, at length, I found that the noise was not within my ears.

No doubt I now grew very pale;—but I talked more fluently, and with a heightened voice. Yet the sound increased—and what could I do? It was a low, dull, quick sound—much such a sound as a watch makes when enveloped in cotton. I gasped for breath—and yet the officers heard it not. I talked more quickly—more vehemently; but the noise steadily increased. I arose and argued about trifles, in a high key and with violent gesticulations; but the noise steadily increased. Why would they not be gone? I paced the floor to and fro with heavy strides, as if excited to fury by the observations of the men—but the noise steadily increased. Oh God! what could I do? I foamed—I raved—I swore! I swung the chair upon which I had been sitting, and grated it upon the boards, but the noise arose over all and continually increased. It grew louder—louder—louder! And still the men chatted pleasantly, and smiled. Was it possible they heard not? Almighty God!—no, no! They heard!—they suspected!—they knew!—they were making a mockery of my horror!-this I thought, and this I think. But anything was better than this agony! Anything was more tolerable than this derision! I could bear those hypocritical smiles no longer! I felt that I must scream or die! and now—again!—hark! louder! louder! louder! louder!

"Villains!" I shrieked, "dissemble no more! I admit the deed!—tear up the planks! here, here!—It is the beating of his hideous heart!"

Source: Museum of Edgar Allan Poe (www.poemuseum.org).

Poetry

The vast output of poetry in the United States during the early republic and antebellum era was as diverse as the new nation itself. Although the field was dominated by several key figures, ranging from Henry Wadsworth Longfellow and Edgar Allan Poe to Emily Dickinson and Walt Whitman, the poetry of the period drew from a great many literary traditions. Perhaps the most obvious feature of American verse during this time was its attempt to break free from the conventions of England's poetic tradition. American poets gradually adopted poetic forms and content specific to the United States and not the "mother country."

Early Influences

One of the greatest influences on early American poetry was Native American oral tradition, as the translation of Native American songs, stories, and verse was a popular fad during the years of the early republic. Creation myths, prayers, nature songs, war songs, and love songs all were key components of Native American poetry, and each of these forms deeply influenced the way American poets produced their own verse. Such influence can be seen in the importance of literary ballads and folk songs to American poetry of the period. Highly rhythmic and melodic, often sentimental, such songs generally celebrated the frontier of the American West, a world that existed outside the bounds of law and decorum. A good example is the popular ballad "The Cowboy's Lament," which begins,

> As I walked out in the streets of Laredo,
> As I walked out in Laredo one day,
> I spied a poor cowboy wrapped up in white linen,
> Wrapped up in white linen as cold as the clay.

Another prominent characteristic of American poetry in these years is its reliance on Christian hymns and spirituals. In particular, it was through this form that American poets, along with slaves themselves, engaged with the experience of slavery. The United States, then as much as now, was largely a Protestant nation, and slave owners felt obligated to instruct their slaves in the Christian tradition in order to spread the biblical notion of obedience. Nevertheless, African slaves were able to find in the Judeo-Christian tradition a number of narratives that they could adapt to their own situation for symbolic and poetic purposes. The Old Testament story of the Jews' deliverance from bondage in Egypt, as well as the New Testament portrayal of Jesus as Christ the redeemer, were frequently appropriated in poems, ballads, hymns, and spirituals, both literary and popular, white and black.

The combination of African and Judeo-Christian narratives influenced not only the content of the poems but also their form. Writers frequently adopted slave dialect, and many spirituals mimed the call-and-response sermon style of American churches—as in "Swing Low, Sweet Chariot," "Ezekiel Saw de Wheel," and "There is a Balm in Gilead," among many others. Although most of these verses were lively, exuberant, and rhythmic, the subject matter obviously was somber.

Bryant and Longfellow

Besides Indian- and Christian-inspired poetry, the early years of the American republic saw a variety of other forms, including children's verse, comic verse, dialect verse, and, as the nineteenth century wore on, both patriotic and protest poetry. Among the literary elite, the poetic output of the United States was dominated by a group of New England writers known as the Fireside Poets, which included William Cullen Bryant, Oliver Wendell Holmes, Henry Wadsworth Longfellow, James Russell Lowell, and John Greenleaf Whittier. The poetry produced by these writers was mostly conventional in form and often sentimental in tone.

Born in Massachusetts in 1794, Bryant was inspired by his early readings of such British poets as Alexander Pope. He began writing verse at a young age and, by the age of 13, had published *The Embargo; or, Sketches of the Times*, an anti–Thomas Jefferson satire. In

1817, Bryant's most famous poem, "Thanatopsis," appeared in the *North American Review,* and he became an instant literary celebrity. Like much of Bryant's later poetry, "Thanatopsis" is a meditation on "Nature's teachings" and represents a new emphasis in American poetry on the environment and natural world. Bryant's other important poems include "To a Waterfowl," "Green River," "Summer Wood," and "Autumn Woods"—titles that likewise reflect the centrality of nature to his poetic style. Not surprisingly, Bryant's affinity for nature also translated into his daily life. In particular, he played a key role in the establishment of New York City's Central Park.

Perhaps the most recognizable of the Fireside Poets, especially for modern readers, is Longfellow. Born in Maine in 1807, he was a classmate of Nathaniel Hawthorne at Bowdoin College. Longfellow went on to become a professor of language and literature at Bowdoin and, eventually, Harvard University. In 1855, he wrote his epic poem *Song of Hiawatha,* one of the best-known works of poetry in American literature. Based on the myths of the Ojibwa Indians, who at the time lived on the shores of Lake Superior, *The Song of Hiawatha* is epic in every sense of the word. The famous opening lines establish both its theme and musical rhythm:

> *By the shores of Gitche Gumee,*
> *By the shining Big-Sea-Water,*
> *Stood the wigwam of Nokomis,*
> *Daughter of the Moon, Nokomis.*

In January 1861, with the states of the Lower South seceding from the Union, Longfellow published another of his most famous poems, "Paul Revere's Ride," in the pages of *The Atlantic Monthly.* The opening lines are as familiar to modern readers as any in American poetry:

> *Listen my children and you shall hear*
> *Of the midnight ride of Paul Revere.*

Longfellow's ballad tells the story of Massachusetts patriot Paul Revere, who on April 18, 1775, took his famous "midnight ride" to warn colonials of advancing British forces. Longfellow wrote the poem on April 19, 1860, the eighty-fifth anniversary of the Battle of Lexington and Concord, which marked the outbreak of the Revolutionary War. Now, on the brink of another major conflict, Longfellow warned again of "the hour of darkness and peril and need." His purpose is clear: to inspire fellow citizens in the fight against slavery and to preserve the Union.

Romanticism and Transcendentalism

Even as American poets were beginning to develop their own native forms, the influence of British literature on their work remained strong. Inspired by the events of the American, French, and Industrial revolutions, British poets such as William Blake, Lord Byron, Samuel Taylor Coleridge, John Keats, Percy Bysshe Shelley, and William Wordsworth took the literary vanguard of a sweeping artistic and intellectual movement known as Romanticism. Like its counterpart in other artistic forms, Romantic poetry stressed a reverence for nature, the human imagination, and strong emotion. The Romanticists, to borrow Wordsworth's phrase, viewed poetry as "the spontaneous overflow of powerful feelings from emotions recollected in tranquility."

The influence of British Romanticism, as well as its French and German counterparts, is especially apparent in the prose and poetry of Edgar Allan Poe and the verse of the Transcendentalists. Although Poe's work—with its dark, supernatural themes and foreboding tone—appears far different from the work of Transcendentalists such as Ralph Waldo Emerson and Henry David Thoreau, all share a common ancestry. Poe was influenced by the Romantics, specifically Byron and Shelley, insofar as he believed that the highest goal of poetry is to arouse intense feelings. This belief is manifested in his haunting verse, particularly the long, incantatory "The Raven," published in 1845. The poem famously begins as a man sits in his study remembering his long-lost love, Lenore. A "stately Raven" thereupon flies into the room, and each time the poet speaks to it, the raven responds with a single word: "Nevermore." The poem was an immediate popular success, making Poe a literary superstar. He was especially revered among the French, as his cryptic verse became an inspiration to the Symbolist poets Charles Baudelaire and Stéphane Mallarmé.

At the same time that Poe was writing his poetry in the Mid-Atlantic region, the Transcendentalist movement was taking shape in New England. Influenced, like Poe, by the Romantic movement, writers such as Amos Bronson Alcott, Emerson, Thoreau, and others began to criticize the predominant religious and secular philosophies of the time. In particular, the Transcendentalists espoused the belief that God can be found everywhere in the immediate world, especially in nature. Most of the Transcendentalists communicated their ideas through essays, but many of them published poetry as well, Emerson most notably. In such poems as "To Rhea," "Hamatreya," "The Rhodora," "Astraea," and "The Snow-Storm," Emerson treated mostly natural themes. In "The Snow-Storm," for example, the language of architecture clashes with the imagery of a blizzard, staging a conflict between industrial development and nature that typified the Transcendentalists' worldview:

> *Come see the north wind's masonry.*
> *Out of an unseen quarry evermore*
> *Furnished with tile, the fierce artificer*
> *Curves his white bastions with projected roof*
> *Round every windward stake, or tree, or door.*

Whitman and Dickinson

When Walt Whitman sent the first edition of his collection of poems, *Leaves of Grass* (1855), to Emerson, the latter acclaimed it as a work of genius. His contemporaries in the literary world and the reading public did not take it as seriously. Over the course of his lifetime, Whitman continually revised and expanded the collection in a succession of ever-expanding editions. Conceived in the throes of American expansion and the Mexican-American War, *Leaves of Grass* represented a new kind of kind of verse, commenting on the changing political climate and the moment-to-moment experiences of ordinary Americans. Influenced by the King James Bible, as well as by the invention of photography, Whitman began crafting *Leaves of Grass* in the 1840s and 1850s, later adding poems that directly addressed the heated political subjects of slavery, President Abraham Lincoln, and the Civil War. Breaking down traditional distinctions between proper and improper subjects for poetry, he purposefully sought to democratize the genre. Eschewing obscure symbols and allegory, Whitman celebrated sensual experience, the body, and the material world. Despite a less-than-stellar literary reputation during his lifetime, within a decade of his death, Whitman was being hailed as the "greatest of all American poets."

Many scholars have granted the same accolade to Emily Dickinson. Born in 1830 in Massachusetts, she spent the majority of her life writing poetry at her family home in Amherst. Dickinson wrote well over 1,700 poems, but few were published during her lifetime. Unlike Whitman's verse, which was expansive, loose, and overtly political, Dickinson's poems tended to be short, lyrical, and filled with dashes and abnormal capitalization. Her famous poem "I Heard a Fly Buzz When I Died" is representative of her style:

> I heard a fly buzz when I died;
> The stillness in the room
> Was like the stillness in the air
> Between the heaves of storm.

It would not be until the 1890s, with the posthumous publication of several editions of her lyrics, that Dickinson would come to be regarded as a preeminent American poet.

American poetry, then, took many directions, both stylistically and thematically, in the first decades of the republic. From the more traditional verse of Longfellow, to the dark and emotive poems of Poe, to the highly sensual work of Whitman and the lyrical, intuitive poems of Dickinson, the nation's poets during this period created an impressive body of work that established a distinctly American tradition. Indeed, it has been argued, there has never been a generation of American poets equal to that of the early republic and antebellum era.

Corey McEleney

See also: Bryant, William Cullen; Emerson, Ralph Waldo; Environment and Nature, Views of; Longfellow, Henry Wadsworth; Lowell, James Russell; Poe, Edgar Allan; Transcendentalism; Whittier, John Greenleaf

◇◇◇

"Wade in the Water," Slave Spiritual, 1830s

◇◇◇

Slave spirituals, religious folk songs with African tribal roots and Christian themes, had a direct influence on mainstream American poetry in the nineteenth century. Many were sung in the rhythmic, call-and-response style of a church sermon, typically in unison, often in a work field. Among the most popular was "Wade in the Water," which took the form shown here in the early 1830s. The song serves as a prime example of why slave owners were leery of allowing their bondsmen to sing. The references to Jesus's baptism in the Jordan and Moses's escape from Egypt hint at redemption and escape. Owners feared that the song contained hidden advice for runaways—by crossing bodies of water, they could hide their tracks from slave catchers.

Wade in the water
Wade in the water, children,
Wade in the water
God's a-going to trouble the water
See that host all dressed in white
God's a-going to trouble the water
The leader looks like the Israelite
God's a-going to trouble the water
See that band all dressed in red
God's a-going to trouble the water
Looks like the band that Moses led
God's a-going to trouble the water
Look over yonder, what do I see?
God's a-going to trouble the water
The Holy Ghost a-coming on me
God's a-going to trouble the water
If you don't believe I've been redeemed
God's a-going to trouble the water
Just follow me down to the Jordan's stream
God's a-going to trouble the water

Source: Gwendolin Sims Warren, *Ev'ry Time I Feel the Spirit: 101 Best-Loved Psalms, Gospel Hymns and Spiritual Songs of the African-American Church* (New York: Henry Holt, 1997).

Theater

In the decades between independence and the Civil War, theater was among the most popular forms of entertainment in the United States. As in many other areas of the nation's cultural life, early theater borrowed heavily from Great Britain. By about the middle of the nineteenth century, however, uniquely American forms of performance began to emerge.

The Early American Stage

In the immediate aftermath of the Revolutionary War, theater was seen by many Americans as too great a symbol of British tyranny and elitism to be trusted; therefore, theatrical performances all but disappeared. As the 1780s came to a close, however, public figures such as William Dunlap, Philip Freneau, and Noah Webster began calling for a "high" culture that differed from, yet rivaled, that of Europe. Webster wrote, "You have been children long enough. You have an empire to raise and support by your exertions and a national character to establish and extend by your wisdom and virtues."

Nevertheless, between the years 1781 and 1825, that "native" culture strongly resembled the cultural productions of Britain. The first production of a play written in the United States was Royall Tyler's *The Contrast* (1787), based on British dramatist Richard Brinsley Sheridan's *The School for Scandal* (1777). The primary difference between the two works was the presence of a character called "Brother Jonathan," a humble but earnest man dressed in a tricornered hat and long military jacket—the garb of an American revolutionary. Initially, the British used Brother Jonathan to lampoon colonists, portraying them as simpleminded rubes. American audiences ultimately embraced

Brother Jonathan as a symbol of their rustic republican honesty and naïveté, as against the wily ways of British urban sophisticates.

The Contrast, and works like it, was an inspiration to early American theater manager and playwright William Dunlap. Embracing the notion that plays could convey a unifying message for Americans, Dunlap strove to inculcate republican "virtue" and patriotism in New York audiences. To their chagrin, however, Dunlap and fellow thespians in Boston and Philadelphia found that this approach did not bring in adequate receipts. Consequently, in order to turn a profit, Dunlap and other theater managers increasingly turned to bombastic—and expensive—depictions of American victories in the recent war. Characteristic of this genre was John Daly Burk's *Bunker Hill; or, Death of General Warren* (1797), which contained much violent action, culminating in the death of the martyr, Warren. This sort of secular "hellfire and brimstone" production followed the lead of British playwright Oliver Goldsmith, who advocated the "enthusiasm" of the Great Awakening pulpit on the theater stage. Dunlap found such techniques "deplorable," but their profitability led him to produce this and similar works.

Melodrama

In the early years of the nineteenth century, melodrama came to dominate the American stage. Shakespearean tragedies such as *Hamlet* and *Macbeth* were wildly popular, as were Gothic melodramas from France, Germany, and Great Britain. Among the most popular and successful imports was *Pizarro in Peru; or, The Death of Rolla* (1800)—a tale of the Incas' desperate last stand against the Spanish. Adapted by Dunlap and Sheridan from the works of German dramatist August von Kotzebue, *Pizarro in Peru* featured a climactic scene in which the hero—Rolla—leaps across a wide chasm with a baby in one hand and a sword in the other. The play was performed across the United States, in one form or another, for more than 70 years.

The success of *Pizarro* and other melodramas fueled a wave of theater building. In 1812, the Walnut Street Theatre in Philadelphia—now America's oldest existing theater—staged its first play, with Thomas Jefferson and the Marquis de Lafayette in attendance. New York followed Philadelphia's lead with the opening of the Anthony Street Theatre the following year. Over the next two decades, a half-

Edwin Booth, portrayed here in the role of Othello, was the premier American actor of the nineteenth century. Shakespearean tragedies dominated the stage through mid-century.

dozen more theaters opened in the area around the Anthony Street Theatre. These venues formed the foundation of the famous theater district that, by the 1850s, would become known as Broadway (after the street that runs through its center).

Theatergoing was not the exclusive privilege of Eastern city dwellers. As the nation expanded across the Appalachian Mountains into Ohio and Kentucky, to Missouri, and into the South, managers presented a mix of melodramas and older British plays. Besides the works of Shakespeare, popular imports included George Lillo's *The London Merchant* (1731), Goldsmith's *She Stoops to Conquer* (1773), and Sheridan's *The School for Scandal* (1777). These were presented alongside such American works as *Bunker*

Hill and *The Contrast,* which remained extremely popular well into the nineteenth century.

For actors who could not work their way into the established companies of the Eastern seaboard, a traveling circuit developed in the West. Included in this circuit were burgeoning cities and towns from Montreal to New Orleans. Some communities built permanent playhouses, others temporarily repurposed churches and other buildings, and still others employed showboats that traveled up and down the Mississippi and other rivers. As the American theater spread to such far-flung venues, and as it adapted to fit the tastes of diverse audiences, it finally took on the uniquely American character that Dunlap, Freneau, and Webster had called for in the 1780s.

Performance and Performers

One the unique elements of American theater in the first decades of the nineteenth century was the manner in which plays were performed. The organization of theaters reflected the class and racial tensions of the period—boxes were reserved for the wealthy, the pit for the middle class, the gallery for the poor, and the seats at the very back for African Americans. Audience behavior was similar to that of a crowd at a modern-day sporting event—shouting at the actors was common, as was loud cheering and booing during scenes. Unhappy audience members also felt free to throw rotten eggs and other objects at performers. After one especially unsatisfactory performance, a reviewer reported, "Cabbages, carrots, pumpkins, potatoes, a wreath of vegetables, a sack of flour and one of soot, and a dead goose, with other articles, simultaneously fell upon the stage."

Americans also favored particular performers—the nineteenth-century version of movie stars. Some, such as Edwin Booth and Edwin Forrest, were native sons. Others, notably Junius Brutus Booth, John Drew, Edmund Kean, and William Charles Macready, were British imports. Working-class audiences tended to embrace Forrest, who was noted for his masculine features and boisterous acting style. Macready, by contrast, was more attuned to upper-class tastes, with his delicate features and more subtle interpretations. The two men developed a heated rivalry that spilled over to their legions of fans. In May 1849, the acrimony culminated in violence as fans of Forrest invaded New York's Astor Place Opera House while Macready was performing. The Astor Place Riot, as the incident became known, resulted in the deaths of 20 people. Macready fled the United States, never to return.

Noble and Ignoble Savages

American theater performances thus took on a rough-hewn and boisterous quality that was unique to and characteristic of the new nation. The 1830s also saw the development of plays based on distinctly American themes and subjects. Native Americans, for example, began finding their way into dramatic works. This was at least in part the result of an 1828 contest organized by Edwin Forrest, who wanted to see more American dramas and fewer British plays. To that end, Forrest offered a prize of $500 and half the third night's proceeds to the playwright who penned the best five-act tragedy featuring a Native American. The winner was John Augustus Stone, whose play *Metamora; or, Last of the Wampanoags* (1829), offered a dramatic interpretation of King Philip's War (1675–1676), pitting Massachusetts Puritans against an Indian coalition led by Wampanoag chief Metacom.

Metamora—as Metacom was renamed in the play—was the first Native American dramatic character to capture a wide audience. As written by Stone and performed by Forrest, Metamora represented a freedom of spirit with which Americans could identify: "The Wampanoag . . . owns no master, save that One who holds the sun in his right hand," intones the work's narrator. The play utilized a feather prized by Metamora to symbolize the soul of North America. The feather is passed on to the most virtuous of the white newcomers, Oceana, who in turn passes it on to the virtuous artisan-yeoman Walter, her beau. The play suggested to American audiences that they were the natural heirs to the "spirit" of North America, as embodied by "noble savages" such as Metamora. It was a runaway success and inspired many imitators to create works around Native American themes. Some employed the noble savage stereotype; many more portrayed native peoples as "ignoble savages"—ruthless and bloodthirsty. They were usually played by white actors in redface makeup.

Blackface Minstrelsy

Another unique development in the American antebellum theater was the emergence of the blackface minstrel show. According to legend, a white actor named Thomas D. "Daddy" Rice met a partially crippled slave near Louisville, Kentucky, while on a theatrical tour. The slave, named Jim Crow, performed a song-and-dance routine while cleaning stables. Rice reportedly learned the song and dance, "blacked up" his face with burnt cork, and performed the routine "to much approbation." Rice refined his show while working with the famed Ludlow and Smith Company, whose producers, Noah Ludlow and Solomon Smith, had something approaching a monopoly on the major stages of the Ohio and Mississippi valleys until the early 1850s. Rice's songs and dances became a featured billing.

Although Rice initially found audiences for his blackface performances in the South and West, the entertainment soon spread across the country. Rice inspired scores of imitators, who further developed the content and style of the minstrel show. Epitomized by companies such as Christy's Minstrels and the Virginia Minstrels, and by performers such as Dan Emmett, the minstrel show was a wild affair of jokes, skits, songs, and dances. It caricatured African American dialect and mannerisms and made extensive use of such stereotypes as the docile Sambo, the crafty Zip Coon, and the matronly Mammy. Much of the popular music of the day came from minstrel shows, including Stephen Foster's songs "Oh! Susanna" (1848), "Massa's in de Cold Ground" (1852), and "My Old Kentucky Home" (1853).

Reform and Theater

At the same time that "redface" and "blackface" performances were appearing on the American stage, theater managers of the antebellum era began presenting plays with a strong reformist message. W.H. Smith's *The Drunkard* (1850), for example, depicted the pathos of a virtuous young man turned ruinous alcoholic. The play concluded with its hero recognizing the negative effect that alcohol has had on his life and pledging abstinence. The message, hardly subtle, was the philosophy of the burgeoning prohibition movement, of which Smith was a member.

Even more influential than *The Drunkard* were the "Tom Shows" based on Harriet Beecher Stowe's best-selling 1852 antislavery novel *Uncle Tom's Cabin.* Stowe, because of her religious convictions, was suspicious of the theater and unwilling to lend her name to any "official" adaptation of the book. That fact, coupled with U.S. copyright law at the time, cleared the way for dozens of authors to develop their own dramatic adaptations. Some of the Tom Shows were more faithful than others to the original novel. All of them drew on minstrelsy, with black characters played by white actors in blackface and presented as broad stereotypes. So popular were these performances that they outlived slavery by many decades.

Tom Shows and other minstrel presentations, along with plays such as *The Drunkard* and *Metamora,* were popular not only in the United States but also in Europe. Webster, Freneau, and Dunlap would have been shocked and disappointed to find that their aspirations for a new "high American art form" had resulted in the development of minstrelsy and melodrama. Yet, by including African Americans, Indians, and the plight and dreams of the "lowly" mechanic and yeoman, a uniquely American art form was, in fact, established. This art form would spread throughout the world and set the stage for other American cultural innovations, such as jazz, film noir, and rock and roll.

Douglas S. Harvey

Thoreau, Henry David

(1817–1862)

Famous for his declaration "I went to the woods because I wished to live deliberately," naturalist and philosopher Henry David Thoreau is remembered as one of the foremost thinkers of the Transcendentalist movement and as the author of two important books of political and social theory, *Civil Disobedience* (1849) and *Walden; or, Life in the Woods* (1854).

Early Years

Born in Concord, Massachusetts, on July 12, 1817, he was the son of Cynthia Dunbar and John Thoreau. For most of his childhood, Thoreau's family experienced financial difficulty; his father worked a variety of odd jobs, laboring as a farmer, a grocer, and a teacher, and eventually operating a pencil factory. In 1833, Thoreau entered Harvard University, where he took courses in Germanic languages, philosophy, mineralogy, anatomy, and the classics. He also studied with Orestes Brownson, who was associated with the nascent Transcendentalist movement—a group of New England writers, intellectuals, and activists who promoted a vision of utopian social progress that would be accomplished by embracing nature and by transcending material desires.

When Thoreau graduated from Harvard University in 1837, the United States had just entered an economic depression that put growing numbers of people out of work. Americans began to wonder whether the new capitalist social order could deliver on its promises of prosperity. Thoreau took up the matter in his Harvard commencement essay, "The Commercial Spirit of Modern Times." Addressing his classmates, the 20-year-old declared, "This world is a place of business. What an infinite bustle! I am awaked almost every night by the panting of the locomotive. It interrupts my dreams. . . . I think that there is nothing, not even crime, more opposed to poetry, to philosophy, ay, to life itself, than this incessant business." Thoreau believed that, in the modern, materialistic world, writers and artists had an especially important role: to preserve basic human values that had been forgotten in the competitive scramble for profit and prestige.

After leaving Harvard in 1837, Thoreau began socializing with various members of the Transcendentalist group. With the formation of the Transcendental Club in Cambridge the previous year, the members had begun disseminating their radical view of society and politics. In addition to Brownson, the group included such luminaries as Amos Bronson Alcott, Ralph Waldo Emerson, Margaret Fuller, Frederick Henry Hedge, Theodore Parker, George Putnam, and Jones Very. Thoreau became especially friendly with Emerson, whose essay *Nature* (1836) helped establish the central tenets of the movement.

In the years following his graduation from Harvard, Thoreau moved back to his hometown of Concord, joining his friend Emerson, who had taken up residence there in 1834. In Concord, Thoreau worked primarily as a teacher. He taught foreign languages and science at a number of schools, including one that he and his brother ran. But he had difficulty accommodating the requirements of the profession—thus, for example, he was dismissed by the board of one school for refusing to flog students as punishment for bad behavior. During this time, at Emerson's urging, Thoreau began to publish regularly in the Transcendentalist journal *The Dial*, mostly poems and essays on natural history. He also worked as a handyman and tutor for the Emerson household.

Civil Disobedience and Walden

In 1845, Thoreau constructed a small cabin on property owned by the Emerson family near Walden Pond in Massachusetts, and he lived in it until 1847. During these two years, he continued to enjoy a vibrant intellectual and social life among the Transcendentalists in Concord. In 1846, Thoreau was arrested for poll-tax evasion—he had refused to pay the tax to express his opposition to slavery and the Mexican-American War—and spent a night in jail. His experiences in jail and his motives for disobeying the government became

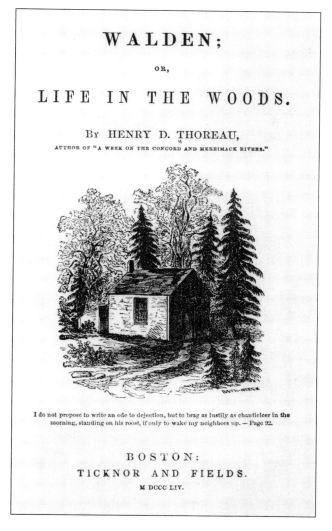

WALDEN;

OR,

LIFE IN THE WOODS.

BY HENRY D. THOREAU,

AUTHOR OF "A WEEK ON THE CONCORD AND MERRIMACK RIVERS."

I do not propose to write an ode to dejection, but to brag as lustily as chanticleer in the morning, standing on his roost, if only to wake my neighbors up. — Page 92.

BOSTON:

TICKNOR AND FIELDS.

M DCCC LIV.

Henry David Thoreau's *Walden* (1854), a memoir of his two-year experiment in "simple living," is at once a critique of industrial society and a manifesto of personal freedom.

the focus of an essay he published as *Resistance to Civil Government* (1849), later retitled *Civil Disobedience*.

One of the first major works of American political philosophy, *Civil Disobedience* argued for the rights of individual citizens and the importance of criticism of, and resistance to, unjust laws. Thoreau's treatise would help shape twentieth-century nonviolent resistance movements, such as Mohandas Gandhi's efforts against British imperialism in South Africa and India and Martin Luther King, Jr.'s protests during the American civil rights movement of the 1950s and 1960s. In his autobiography, King commented on *Civil Disobedience:* "Here, in this courageous New Englander's refusal to pay his taxes and his choice of jail rather than support a war that would spread slavery's territory into Mexico, I made my first contact with the theory of nonviolent resistance."

After leaving Walden Pond in 1847, Thoreau spent the next few years working and writing. In 1849, he published *A Week on the Concord and Merrimack Rivers,* based on a boat trip he had made a decade earlier with his brother John. During these years, Thoreau grew distant from Emerson and worked alternatively as a surveyor and in his family's pencil factory. This period also witnessed Thoreau's growing involvement in the abolitionist movement and his increased interest in natural history. An admirer of evolutionary theorist Charles Darwin, Thoreau wrote avidly in his journal about nature in general and botany in particular.

In 1854, Thoreau published *Walden; or, Life in the Woods.* Presenting his reflections on the two years spent at Walden Pond, the book was a meditation and memoir on "simple living." Anticipating the British philosopher John Stuart Mill's *On Liberty* (1859), *Walden* addressed the ways in which dire economic circumstances create anxieties that prohibit individuals from leading truly free lives. According to Thoreau, his contemporaries were burdened with the obligation to tend to their property, and they suffered because of it. To Thoreau, the people around him were "serfs of the soil . . . so occupied with the fictitious cares and superfluously coarse labors of life that [life's] finer fruits cannot be plucked by them."

Thoreau's primary argument in *Walden* is that the American economic system and what he called "over-civilization" inhibit true liberty, and that breaking free from the tyranny of custom and industrialization is one way of attempting to achieve that liberty. He regarded his own retreat to Walden Pond as an experiment in alternative living that allowed him to question the traditions of previous generations and to cultivate himself through reading and less rigorous labor. According to Thoreau, people experience true liberty when they have the option to experiment not just with a few modes of living but with "a thousand simple tests." Enigmatic, obscure, and rich in symbolism, *Walden* had an immeasurable influence on American writers, social activists, and thinkers of succeeding generations. The book includes some of the most familiar lines in American letters—including one that characterizes Thoreau himself: "If a man does not keep pace with his companions, perhaps it is because he hears the beat of a different drummer."

Later Life and Death

In the years after *Walden,* Thoreau traveled extensively throughout the Northern United States. His observations on nature, which he recorded in the journal he kept for a quarter of a century, were later reworked into lesser-known books of natural history, such as *Autumnal Tints* (1862). He also published several travel narratives.

By the end of the 1850s, Thoreau's political commitments were occupying most of his time. In May 1859, the radical abolitionist John Brown delivered a lecture in Concord attended by Thoreau, Emerson, and other Transcendentalists. Several weeks later, on June 3, 1859, Brown led his infamous raid on Harpers Ferry, Virginia (now West Virginia), in which he attempted to spark a widespread slave revolt. Within 36 hours, Brown and his men were either dead or captured. Brown's actions were the subject of much criticism and consternation, even among members of the Northern abolitionist movement. Thoreau, however, defended Brown's actions. He wrote a lecture titled *A Plea for Captain John Brown,* first given in Concord at the end of October and delivered several times around New England before Brown's December 2 execution. In the lecture, Thoreau recognized Brown as a kindred spirit.

Thoreau's lecture on Brown was one of his last contributions to American public discourse. He had contracted chronic tuberculosis in 1835, and his health declined dramatically in the early years of the Civil War. The author died at home on May 6, 1862. He is buried at Sleepy Hollow Cemetery in Concord, where several members of his Transcendentalist social circle—including Emerson, Hawthorne, and William Ellery Channing—are buried as well. His books *The Maine Woods* and *Cape Cod* were published posthumously, in 1864 and 1865, respectively.

Corey McEleney

See also: Emerson, Ralph Waldo; Environment and Nature, Views of; Transcendentalism

<><><><><><><><><><><><><><><><><><><><><><><><><><><><><><><><>

"Where I Lived, and What I Lived For," *Walden* (excerpt), 1854

<><><><><><><><><><><><><><><><><><><><><><><><><><><><><><><><>

In Henry David Thoreau's classic account of two years living in the woods, Walden, *he offers an idyllic vision of his return to nature and "the essential facts of life." In doing so, Thoreau criticizes the "busyness" of mid-nineteenth-century society and "the lives of quiet desperation" being led by many Americans. In Chapter Two of the book, he describes the setting of his cabin and the values he brought to his life there.*

When first I took up my abode in the woods, that is, began to spend my nights as well as days there, which, by accident, was on Independence Day, or the Fourth of July, 1845, my house was not finished for winter, but was merely a defence against the rain, without plastering or chimney, the walls being of rough, weather-stained boards, with wide chinks, which made it cool at night. The upright white hewn studs and freshly planed door and window casings gave it a clean and airy look, especially in the morning, when its timbers were saturated with dew, so that I fancied that by noon some sweet gum would exude from them. To my imagination it retained throughout the day more or less of this auroral character, reminding me of a certain house on a mountain which I had visited a year before. This was an airy and unplastered cabin, fit to entertain a travelling god, and where a goddess might trail her garments. The winds which passed over my dwelling were such as sweep over the ridges of mountains, bearing the broken strains, or celestial parts only, of terrestrial music. The morning wind forever blows, the poem of creation is uninterrupted; but few are the ears that hear it. Olympus is but the outside of the earth everywhere.

The only house I had been the owner of before, if I except a boat, was a tent, which I used occasionally when making excursions in the summer, and this is still rolled up in my garret; but the boat, after passing from hand to hand, has gone down the stream of time. With this more substantial shelter about me, I had made some progress toward settling in the world. This frame, so slightly clad, was a sort of crystallization around me, and reacted on the builder. It was suggestive somewhat as a picture in outlines. I did not need to go outdoors to take the air, for the atmosphere within had lost none of its freshness. It was not so much within doors as behind a door where I sat, even in the rainiest weather. The Harivansa says, "An abode without birds is like a meat without seasoning." Such was not my abode, for I found myself suddenly neighbor to the birds; not by having imprisoned one, but having caged myself near them. I was not only nearer to some of those which commonly frequent the garden and the orchard, but to those smaller and more thrilling songsters of the forest which never, or rarely, serenade a villager—the wood thrush, the veery, the scarlet tanager, the field sparrow, the whip-poor-will, and many others.

I was seated by the shore of a small pond, about a mile and a half south of the village of Concord and somewhat higher than it, in the midst of an extensive wood between that town and Lincoln, and about two miles south of that our only field known to fame, Concord Battle Ground; but I was so low in the woods that the opposite shore, half a mile off, like the rest, covered with wood, was my most distant horizon. . . .

This small lake was of most value as a neighbor in the intervals of a gentle rain-storm in August, when, both air and water being perfectly still, but the sky overcast, mid-afternoon had all the serenity of evening, and the wood thrush sang around, and was heard from shore to shore. A lake like this is never smoother than at such a time; and the clear portion of the air above it being, shallow and darkened by clouds, the water, full of light and reflections, becomes a lower heaven itself so much the more important. From a hill-top near by, where the wood had been recently cut off, there was a pleasing vista southward across the pond, through a wide indentation in the hills which form the shore there, where their opposite sides sloping toward each other suggested a stream flowing out in that direction through a wooded valley, but stream there was none. That way I looked between and over the near green hills to some distant and higher ones in the horizon, tinged with blue. . . . When I looked across the pond from this peak toward the Sudbury meadows, which in time of flood I distinguished elevated perhaps by a mirage in their seething valley, like a coin in a basin, all the earth beyond the pond appeared like a thin crust insulated and floated even by this small sheet of intervening water, and I was reminded that this on which I dwelt was but *dry land.*

Though the view from my door was still more contracted, I did not feel crowded or confined in the least. There was pasture enough for my imagination. The low shrub oak plateau to which the opposite shore arose stretched away toward the prairies of the West and the steppes of Tartary, affording ample room for all the roving families of men. "There are none happy in the world but beings who enjoy freely a vast horizon," said Damodara, when his herds required new and larger pastures.

Both place and time were changed, and I dwelt nearer to those parts of the universe and to those eras in history which had most attracted me. Where I lived was as far off as many a region viewed nightly by astronomers. We are wont to imagine rare and delectable places in some remote and more celestial corner of the system, behind the constellation of Cassiopeia's Chair, far from noise and disturbance. I discovered that my house actually had its site in such a withdrawn, but forever new and unprofaned, part of the universe. If it were worth the while to settle in those parts near to the Pleiades or the Hyades, to Aldebaran or Altair, then I was really there, or at an equal remoteness from the life which I had left behind, dwindled and twinkling with as fine a ray to my nearest neighbor, and to be seen only in moonless nights by him. . . .

Every morning was a cheerful invitation to make my life of equal simplicity, and I may say innocence, with Nature herself. I have been as sincere a worshipper of Aurora as the Greeks. I got up early and bathed in the pond; that was a religious exercise, and one of the best things which I did. They say that characters were engraven on the bathing tub of King Tching-thang to this effect: "Renew thyself completely each day; do it again, and again, and forever again." I can understand that. Morning brings back the heroic ages. I was as much affected by the faint burn of a mosquito making its invisible and unimaginable tour through my apartment at earliest dawn, when I was sailing with door and windows open, as I

Every morning was a cheerful invitation to make my life of equal simplicity . . . with Nature herself.

could be by any trumpet that ever sang of fame. It was Homer's requiem; itself an Iliad and Odyssey in the air, singing its own wrath and wanderings. There was something cosmical about it; a standing advertisement, till forbidden, of the everlasting vigor and fertility of the world. The morning, which is the most memorable season of the day, is the awakening hour. Then there is least somnolence in us; and for an hour, at least, some part of us awakes which slumbers all the rest of the day and night. Little is to be expected of that day, if it can be called a day, to which we are not awakened by our Genius, but by the mechanical nudgings of some servitor, are not awakened by our own newly acquired force and aspirations from within, accompanied by the undulations of celestial music, instead of factory bells, and a fragrance filling the air—to a higher life than we fell asleep from; and thus the darkness bear its fruit, and prove itself to be good, no less than the light. That man who does not believe that each day contains an earlier, more sacred, and auroral hour than he has yet profaned, has despaired of life, and is pursuing a descending and darkening way. After a partial cessation of his sensuous life, the soul of man, or its organs rather, are reinvigorated each day, and his Genius tries again what noble life it can make. All memorable events, I should say, transpire in morning time and in a morning atmosphere. . . . To him whose elastic and vigorous thought keeps pace with the sun, the day is a perpetual morning. It matters not what the clocks say or the attitudes and labors of men. Morning is when I am awake and there is a dawn in me. Moral reform is the effort to throw off sleep. Why is it that men give so poor an account of their day if they have not been slumbering? They are not such poor calculators. If they had not been overcome with drowsiness, they would have performed something. The millions are awake enough for physical labor; but only one in a million is awake enough for effective intellectual exertion, only one in a hundred millions to a poetic or divine life. To be awake is to be alive. I have never yet met a man who was quite awake. How could I have looked him in the face? . . .

I went to the woods because I wished to live deliberately, to front only the essential facts of life, and see if I could not learn what it had to teach, and not, when I came to die, discover that I had not lived. I did not wish to live what was not life, living is so dear; nor did I wish to practice resignation, unless it was quite necessary. I wanted to live deep and suck out all the marrow of life, to live so sturdily and Spartan-like as to put to rout all that was not life, to cut a broad swath and shave close, to drive life into a corner, and reduce it to its lowest terms, and, if it proved to be mean, why then to get the whole and genuine meanness of it, and publish its meanness to the world; or if it were sublime, to know it by experience, and be able to give a true account of it in my next excursion. For most men, it appears to me, are in a strange uncertainty about it, whether it is of the devil or of God, and have somewhat hastily concluded that it is the chief end of man here to "glorify God and enjoy him forever."

Still we live meanly, like ants; though the fable tells us that we were long ago changed into men; like pygmies we fight with cranes; it is error upon error, and clout upon clout, and our best virtue has for its occasion a superfluous and evitable wretched-ness. Our life is frittered away by detail. An honest man has hardly need to count more than his ten fingers, or in extreme cases he may add his ten toes, and lump the rest. Simplicity, simplicity, simplicity! I say, let your affairs be as two or three, and not a hundred or a thousand; instead of a million count half a dozen, and keep your accounts on your thumb-nail. In the midst of this chopping sea of civilized life, such are the clouds and storms and quicksands and thousand-and-one items to be allowed for, that a man has to live, if he would not founder and go to the bottom and not make his port at all, by dead reckoning, and he must be a great calculator indeed who succeeds. Simplify, simplify. Instead of three meals a day, if it be necessary eat but one; instead of a hundred dishes, five; and reduce other things in proportion. . . .

The nation itself, with all its so-called internal improvements, which, by the way are all external and superficial, is just such an unwieldy and overgrown establishment, cluttered with furniture and tripped up by its own traps, ruined by luxury and heedless expense, by want of calculation and a worthy aim, as the million households in the land; and the only cure for it, as for them, is in a rigid economy, a stern and more than Spartan simplicity of life and elevation of purpose. It lives too fast. Men think that it is essential that the Nation have commerce, and export ice, and talk through a telegraph, and ride thirty miles an hour, without a doubt, whether they do or not; but whether we should live like baboons or like men, is a little uncertain. If we do not get out sleepers, and forge rails, and devote days and nights to the work, but go to tinkering upon our lives to improve them, who will build railroads? And if railroads are not built, how shall we get to heaven in season? But if we stay at home and mind our business, who will want railroads? We do not ride on the railroad; it rides upon us. Did you ever think what those sleepers are that underlie the railroad? Each one is a man, an Irishman, or a Yankee man. The rails are laid on them, and they are covered with sand, and the cars run smoothly over them. They are sound sleepers, I assure you. And every few years a new lot is laid down and run over; so that, if some have the pleasure of riding on a rail, others have the misfortune to be ridden upon. And when they run over a man that is walking in

> The nation itself, with all its so-called internal improvements, . . . is just such an unwieldy and overgrown establishment.

his sleep, a supernumerary sleeper in the wrong position, and wake him up, they suddenly stop the cars, and make a hue and cry about it, as if this were an exception. I am glad to know that it takes a gang of men for every five miles to keep the sleepers down and level in their beds as it is, for this is a sign that they may sometime get up again.

Why should we live with such hurry and waste of life? We are determined to be starved before we are hungry. Men say that a stitch in time saves nine, and so they take a thousand stitches today to save nine tomorrow. . . . Hardly a man takes a half-hour's nap after dinner, but when he wakes he holds up his head and asks, "What's the news?" as if the rest of mankind had stood his sentinels. Some give directions to be waked every half-hour, doubtless for no other purpose; and then, to pay for it, they tell what they have dreamed. After a night's sleep the news is as indispensable as the breakfast. . . .

For my part, I could easily do without the post-office. I think that there are very few important communications made through it. To speak critically, I never received more than one or two letters in my life—I wrote this some years ago—that were worth the postage. The penny-post is, commonly, an institution through which you seriously offer a man that penny for his thoughts which is so often safely offered in jest. And I am sure that I never read any memorable news in a newspaper. If we read of one man robbed, or murdered, or killed by accident, or one house burned, or one vessel wrecked, or one steamboat blown up, or one cow run over on the Western Railroad, or one mad dog killed, or one lot of grasshoppers in the winter—we never need read of another. One is enough. If you are acquainted with the principle, what do you care for a myriad instances and applications? . . .

Shams and delusions are esteemed for soundest truths, while reality is fabulous. If men would steadily observe realities only, and not allow themselves to be deluded, life, to compare it with such things as we know, would be like a fairy tale and the Arabian Nights' Entertainments. If we respected only what is inevitable and has a right to be, music and poetry would resound along the streets. When we are unhurried and wise, we perceive that only great and worthy things have any permanent and absolute existence, that petty fears and petty pleasures are but the shadow of the reality. This is always exhilarating and sublime. By closing the eyes and slumbering, and consenting to be deceived by shows, men establish and confirm their daily life of routine and habit everywhere, which still is built on purely illusory foundations. Children, who play life, discern its true law and relations more clearly than men, who fail to live it worthily, but who think that they are wiser by experience, that is, by failure. . . . I perceive that we inhabitants of New England live this mean life that we do because our vision does not penetrate the surface of things. We think that that is which appears to be. . . .

Let us spend one day as deliberately as Nature, and not be thrown off the track by every nutshell and mosquito's wing that falls on the rails. Let us rise early and fast, or break fast, gently and without perturbation; let company come and let company go, let the bells ring and the children cry—determined to make a day of it. Why should we knock under and go with the stream? Let us not be upset and overwhelmed in that terrible rapid and whirlpool called a dinner, situated in the meridian shallows. Weather this danger and you are safe, for the rest of the way is down hill. With unrelaxed nerves, with morning vigor, sail by it, looking another way, tied to the mast like Ulysses. If the engine whistles, let it whistle till it is hoarse for its pains. If the bell rings, why should we run? We will consider what kind of music they are like. Let us settle ourselves, and work and wedge our feet downward through the mud and slush of opinion, and prejudice, and tradition, and delusion, and appearance, that alluvion which covers the globe, through Paris and London, through New York and Boston and Concord, through Church and State, through poetry and philosophy and religion, till we come to a hard bottom and rocks in place, which we can call reality, and say, This is, and no mistake. . . . If you stand right fronting and face-to-face to a fact, you will see the sun glimmer on both its surfaces, as if it were a cimeter, and feel its sweet edge dividing you through the heart and marrow, and so you will happily conclude your mortal career. Be it life or death, we crave only reality. If we are really dying, let us hear the rattle in our throats and feel cold in the extremities; if we are alive, let us go about our business.

Time is but the stream I go a-fishing in. I drink at it; but while I drink I see the sandy bottom and detect how shallow it is. Its thin current slides away, but eternity remains. I would drink deeper; fish in the sky, whose bottom is pebbly with stars. I cannot count one. I know not the first letter of the alphabet. I have always been regretting that I was not as wise as the day I was born. The intellect is a cleaver; it discerns and rifts its way into the secret of things. I do not wish to be any more busy with my hands than is necessary. My head is hands and feet. I feel all my best faculties concentrated in it. My instinct tells me that my head is an organ for burrowing, as some creatures use their snout and fore paws, and with it I would mine and burrow my way through these hills. I think that the richest vein is somewhere hereabouts; so by the divining-rod and thin rising vapors I judge; and here I will begin to mine.

Sources: The Walden Woods Project (www.walden.org); *The Writings of Henry David Thoreau* (Walden edition), 20 vols. (Boston: Houghton Mifflin, 1906).

Transcendentalism

America's first indigenous philosophical movement, Transcendentalism emerged in the late 1820s out of the writings and discussions of a small cadre of New England Unitarian ministers, social reformers, and intellectuals, most notably Amos Bronson Alcott, Orestes Brownson, Ralph Waldo Emerson, Margaret Fuller, Nathaniel Hawthorne, and Henry David Thoreau. Emphasizing independence of thought and the importance of everyday experience in shaping perception, the movement reached its productive and influential peak between the mid-1830s and late 1850s.

The Transcendentalist movement can be understood as an idealist reaction against British empiricism (the idea that all knowledge comes from the senses, reason, and reflection on experience), as well as a turning against the dominant Protestant doctrine, secular intellectualism, and the early Industrial Revolution. As such, it emphasized the innate, intuitive power of the human mind, a spiritual state that transcends the material plane, the immanence (pervasiveness) of the divine, and the moral insight and creative energy of the individual.

Yet the movement remained amorphous and protean (diverse, varied in form), drawing from a number of sources and lacking any formal declaration of principles. In part because of this, it profoundly influenced American culture in its time and for generations to come. Its adherents and the ideals of the movement affected virtually every realm of nineteenth-century culture, including literature and the arts, religion, politics, and social reform activities. By the start of the Civil War, Transcendentalism was less vital as a distinct philosophy, though it continued to influence American culture and thinking in profound ways.

Ideological Origins and Core Concepts

The Transcendentalist movement derived fundamentally from the philosophical assertion—drawn from the work of the German philosopher Immanuel Kant—that individuals are born with some knowledge and understanding. This idea directly challenged the pervasive view that knowledge can be gained only through the senses. For the Transcendentalists, an individual's mind actively shapes and inherently values certain basic ideals. Moving beyond a strict reading of Kant, the Transcendentalists also held that an individual can gain access to essential truths through the revelation provided by everyday life, objects, and experiences. In addition to Kantian philosophy—which American Transcendentalists became familiar with through the writings of Thomas Carlyle, Samuel Coleridge, and other European writers—a variety of other philosophies and belief systems, including Eastern religions, Platonism, Romanticism, Swedenborgianism, and Unitarianism, helped shape the Transcendentalist movement.

Although Transcendentalism drew most of its inspiration from European and Asian thought, the movement was distinctly American. Like the nation itself, the movement placed fundamental importance on principles of individualism, idealism, and democracy. If ideas are inherent in every person, Transcendentalists reasoned, then individuals do not need authorities or institutions to control them or to make decisions on their behalf. Beyond that, Transcendentalism emphasized and celebrated individual creative potential and the power of individuals to control their own lives, initiate social change, and achieve greater moral and intellectual enlightenment.

The first stirrings of Transcendentalist thought emerged out of the Unitarian Church, in particular ministers such as William Ellery Channing, Emerson, and George Ripley. These men continued to push Unitarianism away from Calvinism and toward a faith based on experience rather than doctrine. Transcendentalists went so far as to believe that God exists in the human soul. They rejected the divinity of Christ, or at least the uniqueness of his divinity, and understood Jesus as a man who recognized the holiness in all people.

If there was any central idea in Transcendentalism, it was this: There is divinity in all persons and in all of nature, and this divinity connects everything and is readily accessible through intuition and reflection. This core concept found its most direct expression in Emerson's essay "Nature" (1836), in which he argued that nature is divine and that human beings, as part of nature, inherently embody this divinity and need only to open themselves to recognize it.

Although the Transcendentalist movement had no formal structure, two institutions provided a venue for the development and dissemination of its ideas. Founded in 1836 by Emerson, Frederick Henry Hedge, George Putnam, and Ripley, the Transcendental Club in Cambridge, Massachusetts, was the first. Organizers sought an informal gathering place for new ideas and spirited intellectual discussions in response to what they viewed as the vapid culture of nearby Harvard College and of America more generally. Over four years, the group held some 30 meetings, with many of New England's leading liberal lights, including a number of women, attending at one time or another.

The other Transcendentalist enterprise, a journal called *The Dial*, was launched in 1840, the year in which the club ceased meeting. Members founded *The Dial* because most existing journals refused or rarely accepted Transcendentalist writings. Margaret Fuller served as the first editor until 1842; Emerson took over thereafter, laboring two years until the journal's dissolution in 1844. Although *The Dial* never succeeded financially, it provided an important public venue for Transcendentalist ideas and writings.

Literary Efforts, Political Philosophy, Social Reform

In addition to shared philosophical concepts, Transcendentalism was defined by a vibrant and diverse literary movement; many of the leading Transcendentalists wrote and published prose and poetry. Emerson's essays and Thoreau's writings rank among the best of American letters, and the movement as a whole has had an enduring influence on the national literature. One of the hallmarks of Transcendentalist writings is the ability to delight and find significance in the mundane, as Thoreau does repeatedly in *Walden; or, Life in the Woods* (1854). The best Transcendentalist writing also uses structure and language as a means of conveying meaning and insight. In *Walden*, for example, the seasonal organization of the book emphasizes the regeneration that Thoreau experienced through the economy he practiced and the nature he communed with at the pond. In Emerson's writings, words and their origins themselves suggest a series of connections that reinforce the themes of his essays. These aspects of Transcendentalist literature influenced such contemporaries as Emily Dickinson, Herman Melville, and Walt Whitman, as well as countless later authors.

Another unifying factor among the Transcendentalists was shared political principles. As a group, they were intensely committed to individual liberty and democracy, taking a broadly libertarian position against the regulation of society by the state. At the same time, the Transcendentalists looked askance at property protections and shunned the economic self-interest that generally accompanied many nineteenth-century Americans' devotion to liberty. Instead, they supported communal endeavors that presaged twentieth-century liberalism. Despite their shared values, Transcendentalists did not uniformly support either the Whig or the Democratic Party. Believing that neither party truly embodied their beliefs, many stood aloof from public involvement in electoral politics.

This hardly meant that they recoiled from politics or from engaging in pressing social concerns. Rather than turn to the formal political process, many of the Transcendentalists attempted to bring their idealism to bear on contemporary affairs through protest and reform efforts. Thoreau's 1849 essay *Civil Disobedience* epitomized the group's resistance to injustice. Paramount among their social causes was abolitionism, as their belief in the inherent divinity of every human being implied a corresponding faith in the equality of all. Most Transcendentalists strongly opposed slavery, contributing time, money, and ideological support to the abolitionist movement. Education reform was another area of concern, as Amos Bronson Alcott and Elizabeth Palmer Peabody, in particular, rejected the rote learning prevalent in mid-nineteenth-century schools and urged an organic approach to developing the intrinsic intellect, imagination, and moral judgment of children.

Dissolution and Influence

By the Civil War, the Transcendentalist movement was conspicuously on the wane. In some ways, the cataclysm of war shocked and realigned all of American culture, hastening the decline of the movement. Death claimed a number of the leading Transcendentalists, including Fuller and Thoreau, while others distanced themselves ideologically. Brownson embraced Catholicism, while Hawthorne became openly critical of the movement. Another reason for the demise of Transcendentalism as a serious, evolving intellectual and literary movement was precisely its widespread influence. Its essential outlook—stressing the inherent intelligence and equality of every person and the power of individual will and experience—already had permeated American culture.

The Transcendentalist movement continued to influence American culture and intellectual life for many generations to come. Its emphasis on personal experience and intuition helped shape the late-nineteenth-century philosophical movement called pragmatism. Likewise, the Beats of the 1950s and the counterculture of the 1960s both drew implicitly and explicitly from the Transcendentalist belief in the holiness inherent in nature and every person and, consequently, shared in the Transcendentalists' celebration of the sublime in the ordinary.

Jeffrey Kosiorek

See also: Emerson, Ralph Waldo; Environment and Nature, Views of; Fuller, Margaret; Thoreau, Henry David

◇◇

Sidelight

Brook Farm, Fruitlands, and Satire

At the same time that they explored new philosophical ideas and urged social reforms, several of the Transcendentalists also sought an alternative social model in utopian communities. The most successful of these cooperative settlements, called Brook Farm, was established by former Unitarian minister George Ripley and his wife Sophia in 1841, just outside Boston in the town of West Roxbury. Ripley and his fellow settlers based the social and economic organization of the collective on a philosophy called Fourierism, after the French social theorist Charles Fourier. Every member of the commune engaged in manual labor, which was intended to stimulate and balance mental pursuits. Additionally, members sought to support each other economically and spiritually, providing an example of humane relations for society at large. Many of those who participated in Brook Farm found their experiences rewarding and drew inspiration from the community. Buoyed by its financially successful schools for children, Brook Farm functioned effectively for about five years, though its agricultural and manufacturing pursuits lost money. The cooperative began falling into decline by 1845 and finally closed in 1847 because of mounting debts.

Reactions to the experiment had been mixed from the beginning, among outsiders, non-participating Transcendentalists, and even community members. One New York newspaper feared that the community was "secretly and industriously aiming to destroy the foundation of society." Ralph Waldo Emerson, who declined to join and questioned the model from the outset, later denounced Brook Farm in his essay collection *The Conduction of Life* (1860). And Henry David Thoreau, after a visit in 1841, wrote in his journal, "As for these communities, I think I had rather keep a bachelor's room in Hell than go to board in Heaven."

Most scathing of all was the indictment of Nathaniel Hawthorne, who was an early member and served as treasurer of the community before leaving in disillusionment after a few months. His novel of 1852, *The Blithedale Romance*, was set in a utopian community based on Brook Farm—as Hawthorne plainly acknowledges in the Preface. With satiric contempt, he mocks the blithe injustice of a community in which some members spend their time reading poetry while others tend cows, and, as in Chapter Eight, the naive optimism of participants who sought redemption or enlightenment in ordinary farmwork.

> While our enterprise lay all in theory, we had pleased ourselves with delectable visions of the spiritualization of labor. It was to be our form of prayer and ceremonial of worship. Each stroke of

the hoe was to uncover some aromatic root of wisdom, heretofore hidden from the sun. Pausing in the field, to let the wind exhale the moisture from our foreheads, we were to look upward, and catch glimpses into the far-off soul of truth. In this point of view, matters did not turn out quite so well as we anticipated. . . . The clods of earth, which we so constantly belabored and turned over and over, were never etherealized into thought. Our thoughts, on the contrary, were fast becoming cloddish. Our labor symbolized nothing, and left us mentally sluggish in the dusk of the evening. Intellectual activity is incompatible with any large amount of bodily exercise. The yeoman and the scholar—the yeoman and the man of finest moral culture, though not the man of sturdiest sense and integrity—are two distinct individuals, and can never be melted or welded into one substance.

Another Transcendentalist experiment in utopian communal living, called Fruitlands, was founded in June 1843 by Amos Bronson Alcott and Charles Lane on 90 acres of farmland in Harvard, Massachusetts, about 25 miles northwest of Boston. A more radical version of Brook Farm, which Alcott regarded as not "austere enough," Fruitlands was committed to raising vegan fare solely by the work of members' own hands; utilizing appropriated labor—including that of draft animals—was forbidden. The goal of participants was to live entirely independent of the outside world and to grow only enough pure crops to feed themselves, so that they could focus their attention on higher, spiritual matters. The community survived less than seven months, closing in December 1843. As literary fate would have it, Fruitland's legacy would be sealed by a child of the founder, Louisa May Alcott, who lived at the community and grew up to become a highly successful author, most notably of the children's classic *Little Women* (1868). Her scores of other works included a highly insightful, bitingly satiric memoir of the short-lived Fruitlands community, *Transcendental Wild Oats* (1873). In the opening section, two of the "modern pilgrims" who found the utopia summarize their ideal:

"Ordinary secular farming is not our object. Fruit, grain, pulse, herbs, flax, and other vegetable products, receiving assiduous attention, will afford ample manual occupation, and chaste supplies for the bodily needs. It is intended to adorn the pastures with orchards, and to supersede the labor of cattle by the spade and the pruning-knife.

"Consecrated to human freedom, the land awaits the sober culture of devoted men. Beginning with small pecuniary means, this enterprise must be rooted in a reliance on the succors of an ever-bounteous Providence, whose vital affinities being secured by this union with uncorrupted field and unworldly persons, the cares and injuries of a life of gain are avoided.

"The inner nature of each member of the Family is at no time neglected. Our plan contemplates all such disciplines, cultures, and habits as evidently conduce to the purifying of the inmates.

"Pledged to the spirit alone, the founders anticipate no hasty or numerous addition to their numbers. The kingdom of peace is entered only through the gates of self-denial; and felicity is the test and the reward of loyalty to the unswerving law of Love."

This prospective Eden at present consisted of an old red farm-house, a dilapidated barn, many acres of meadow-land, and a grove. Ten ancient apple-trees were all the "chaste supply" which the place offered as yet; but, in the firm belief that plenteous orchards were soon to be evoked from their inner consciousness, these sanguine founders had christened their domain Fruitlands.

Like its real-life namesake, the Fruitlands of Alcott's satire collapsed with the onset of winter, its food supplies depleted. "Poor Fruitlands! The name was as great a failure as the rest!" sighs Abel, a thinly disguised personification of Alcott's father. His wife replies: "Don't you think Apple Slump would be a better name for it, dear?"

Webster, Noah

(1758–1843)

Teacher, lawyer, essayist, newspaper editor, reformer, and lexicographer, Noah Webster is best known as the author of *The American Spelling Book* (1783) and the *American Dictionary of the English Language* (1828). He devoted his life to setting down the differences between the language of the American colonies and the language of England. "Our honor requires us to have a system of our own, in language as well as government," he wrote.

Webster was born in West Hartford, Connecticut, on October 16, 1758. His parents, Noah and Mercy Steele Webster, were farmers. Little is known of his life prior to 1774, when he entered Yale College, but his father apparently mortgaged the family farm in order to afford tuition. At Yale, Webster made a number of influential friends, including the poet Joel Barlow, educator Josiah Meigs, and Oliver Wolcott, Jr., who would serve as the second U.S. secretary of the treasury. These social contacts would prove crucial to his future success.

Webster was a devoted Patriot, serving two brief stints in the colonial militia. Although his third year of classes was interrupted by the Revolutionary War, he graduated in 1778 and returned to the family farm, having no other prospects for employment. He soon feuded with his father, who expected him to find a profession and repay his debt. Essentially disowned, Webster had little contact with his parents after 1778. Penniless, he briefly tried teaching as a profession in Glastonbury, Connecticut. He then took a position in Hartford as an aide to Oliver Ellsworth, later chief justice of the U.S. Supreme Court, under whom he read law. Webster was admitted to the bar in 1781, but the financial crisis of the time forced him back to teaching to supplement his income.

It was during his second stint as a teacher that Webster began the project that would solve his financial woes and become his life's work:

Noah Webster earned the nickname "Schoolmaster of the Republic"—the title of this lithograph—for compiling the first books on American spelling, usage, and grammar.

producing textbooks to promote a standardized American language. Many late-eighteenth-century thinkers believed that national identity rested on a shared language. From this perspective, the heterogeneous new nation—with its many accents, diverse spellings of words, and regional slang terms—faced a major problem. For the new republic to survive and become truly independent, Webster believed, children must be taught a distinctively *American* form of English that would be used by all citizens in every region of the country.

To this end, he authored a three-part series of textbooks called *A Grammatical Institute of the English Language* (1783–1785). The first volume, popularly known as "the blue-back speller," was an immediate commercial success and provided Webster with much of his income for the remainder of his life. With sales estimated to exceed 100 million copies by the close of the nineteenth century, his little blue book taught generations of schoolchildren how to spell. The second volume in Webster's series of textbooks focused on grammar and emphasized American usage rather than English tradition. The third volume, a basic reader, introduced American children to excerpts from classic works of literature, including *Hamlet* and *Macbeth*, as well as the republic's foundational political documents.

Webster's texts made him a nationally recognized expert on education, which afforded him the opportunity to lecture and write on a wide array of topics—education reform, medicine, Greek mythology, law, foreign affairs, social reform, and politics. He was a leading proponent of the U.S. Constitution in the Pennsylvania ratification debate, and he launched a short-lived Federalist newspaper, the *American Magazine,* in New York City in 1788.

In 1789, Webster married Rebecca Greenleaf, with whom he would have eight children, and moved to Hartford, where he practiced law and participated in a number of social and literary societies. Among these was an abolitionist society he helped organize in 1791; Webster would support the cause of abolition, along with other social and moral reforms, throughout the rest of his life. Two years later, he returned with his family to New York City and again tried his hand at journalism, editing the pro-Federalist daily *American Minerva* and a semiweekly newspaper called *The Herald.* In 1798, he moved the family to New Haven, Connecticut, where he spent the rest of his life working on his magnum opus, a dictionary of the American language.

Webster's first lexicographical work, *A Compendious Dictionary of the English Language* (1806), incorporated many Americanisms not found in other dictionaries; it contained some 5,000 words more than Samuel Johnson's *A Dictionary of the English Language* (1755), the most popular dictionary in England and America at the time. But the *Compendious* was only a precursor to Webster's remarkable *American Dictionary of the English Language,* published in 1828, which contained definitions of some 70,000 words—30,000 more than any previous dictionary. Embracing nonliterary terms and colloquial expressions, and favoring American usage and pronunciation over British, the work made Webster's name virtually synonymous with "dictionary" in the United States. His simplified system of spelling replaced British forms with more phonetic spellings that became standard "American," such as "honor" rather than "honour" and "plow" rather than "plough."

He also introduced such distinctively American words as "skunk," "hickory," and "chowder."

After publication of the *American Dictionary,* Webster remained active in education and reform causes, always guided by his staunch Federalist principles. He died at his home in New Haven on May 28, 1843, shortly after completing a revision of his dictionary. Webster's death brought a bitter dispute over the literary rights to his work, which was settled in favor of his publishers, George and Charles Merriam. The Merriam Company retained the exclusive rights to the Webster name until the 1950s, even though later editions of the dictionary shed most of Noah Webster's distinctive voice. Regardless, he has had an incalculable influence on American education and language for centuries.

James Rohrer

An American Dictionary of the English Language (excerpts), 1828

In 1828, Noah Webster produced his magnum opus, An American Dictionary of the English Language. *With more than 70,000 words, the dictionary helped standardize American English while also making clear that the language spoken in the United States was distinct from that spoken in Great Britain. Although Webster essentially invented the modern dictionary, he was somewhat more inclined to editorialize than were modern lexicographers, as these sample definitions suggest.*

REVENGE, n. revenj'.

1. Return of an injury; the deliberate infliction of pain or injury [on] a person in return for an injury received from him.

2. According to modern usage, a malicious or spiteful infliction of pain or injury, contrary to the laws of justice and christianity, in return for an injury or offense. Revenge is dictated by passion; vengeance by justice.

3. The passion which is excited by an injury done or an affront given; the desire of inflicting pain on one who has done an injury; as, to glut revenge.

Revenge, as the word is now understood, is always contrary to the precepts of Christ.

The indulgence of revenge tends to make men more savage and cruel.

SLAVE-TRADE, n. [slave and trade.] The barbarous and wicked business of purchasing men and women, transporting them to a distant country and selling them for slaves.

WOMAN, n. plu. women. [a compound of womb and man.]

1. The female of the human race, grown to adult years.

And the rib, which the Lord god had taken from the man, made he a woman. Genesis 2.

Women are soft, mild, pitiful, and flexible.

We see every day women perish with infamy, by having been too willing to set their beauty to show.

I have observed among all nations that the women ornament themselves more t[h]an the men; that wherever found, they are the same kind, civil, obliging, humane, tender beings, inclined to be gay and cheerful, timorous and modest.

2. A female attendant or servant.

WOMAN, v.t. To make pliant.

Sources: Internet Archive (http://archive.org); Noah Webster, *An American Dictionary of the English Language* (New York: S. Converse, 1828).

Whittier, John Greenleaf

(1807–1892)

Poet, editor, essayist, and abolitionist John Greenleaf Whittier was a dedicated Quaker known for his nostalgic poems and popular hymns and for his contributions to the nineteenth-century antislavery movement. He was a member of the Fireside Poets, a group of New Englanders—also including William Cullen Bryant, Oliver Wendell Holmes, Henry David Longfellow, and James Russell Lowell—whose largely conventional verse on patriotic themes, domestic life, and picturesque scenery made them as popular as any poets in Britain. Whittier's reputation lies primarily on such poems as the idyllic Vermont narrative "Snow-Bound" (1866) and the patriotic Civil War ballad "Barbara Fritchie" (1863) and such hymns as "Dear Lord and Father of Mankind" (from his 1872 poem "The Brewing of Soma").

John Greenleaf Whittier was born on a farm near Haverhill, Massachusetts, on December 17, 1807. As the second of four children and the eldest son, he spent much of his childhood laboring on the family farm. The Whittiers, who had lived in the area since the early seventeenth century, attended Quaker meetings in nearby Amesbury. Whittier's formal education was meager, consisting of brief stints at the district school in 1814–1815 and in 1821, when his teacher lent him a book by the Scottish poet Robert Burns.

Until this point, Whittier's reading had been limited almost entirely to the Bible and his father's library of six Quaker books. Determined to become a poet, the boy began scribbling verse with a passion, ignoring his father's warning that he could never earn a living as a writer. Whittier wrote tirelessly at night, spending his days as a teacher and cobbler to raise money for more schooling. Burns was and remained a major influence on his poetry.

In 1826, without Whittier's knowledge, his sister Mary sent his poem "The Exile's Departure" to William Lloyd Garrison, the young editor of the *Free Press* in Newburyport, Massachusetts. Garrison published the poem and encouraged Whittier to send more. The two young men, who shared a love of literature and a common moral vision, soon became friends. Encouraged by Garrison, Whittier enrolled at the Haverhill Academy in 1827 and earned a high school diploma in only one year.

In 1829, Garrison introduced Whittier to the Reverend William Collier, a Boston moral reformer who owned several newspapers and needed a new editor for the weekly *American Manufacturer.* That job, which paid $9 a week plus free board, was the first in a succession of editorial positions Whittier would hold over the next 30 years, including stints at the *New England Weekly Review* (1830–1832), the *Essex Gazette* (1836), the *Pennsylvania Freeman* (1838–1840), the *Middlesex Standard* (1844–1845), and the *National Era* (1847–1859).

Whittier's deep Quaker commitment to pacifism and tolerance, coupled with his close friendship with Garrison, led him to embrace the abolitionist cause with unwavering passion. His political commitment and literary gifts flowed together in the decades leading up to the Civil War; for Whittier, there was no distinction between his role as poet and his commitment to social justice. Publishing primarily in his own papers and Garrison's *The Liberator,* he produced a constant stream of verse, much of it political. Among Whittier's literary and journalistic targets were proslavery politicians and gag rules aimed at silencing abolitionism; the annexation of Texas and the Mexican-American War; the Compromise of 1850 and fugitive slave legislation. He especially assailed churches and clergy who supported slavery or opposed abolition. Among his most acclaimed antislavery poems was "Ichabod" (1850), penned in response to Senator Daniel Webster's unexpected defection from the antislavery movement to support the Compromise of 1850. Other notable poems of the antebellum period include "Maud Muller" (1854) and "The Barefoot Boy" (1855).

In June 1833, at Garrison's persistent urgings, Whittier publicly committed himself to immediate and full abolition in a pamphlet titled *Justice and Expediency,* which attacked the American Colonization Society and its campaign to free the slaves but return them to Africa. Later that year, Whittier served as a delegate to the founding convention of the American Anti-Slavery Society in Philadelphia. He broke with Garrison in 1840 when the movement split over the issue of tactics; Whittier sided with those who sought to advance abolition through political means. As a supporter of the new American and Foreign Anti-Slavery Society, he poured his energy into electing anti-slavery candidates to office. In the aftermath of the Kansas-Nebraska Act of 1854, he played an active role in founding and boosting the new Republican Party.

A committed pacifist, Whittier nevertheless strongly supported President Abraham Lincoln and the Union cause in the Civil War. He greeted the Thirteenth Amendment, which ended slavery, with the joyous hymn "Laus Deo." When the war was over, with emancipation at last a reality, Whittier turned away from politics and devoted himself entirely to literary endeavors. During the remaining four decades of his life, he produced a steady stream of poems, many of them on regional New England themes.

Whittier never married, living from 1876 to the end of his life with cousins near Danvers, Massachusetts. He died in Hampton Falls, New Hampshire, on September 7, 1892, after suffering a paralytic stroke. He was buried in Amesbury, where generations of his family had attended Quaker meetings.

James Rohrer

See also: Poetry

◇◇◇

"Snow-Bound: A Winter Idyl" (excerpt), 1866

◇◇◇

Written as a simple third-person narrative with a relaxed, steady rhythm in rhymed pairs, "Snow-Bound," Whittier's most beloved and critically acclaimed poem, evokes the power and beauty of nature and the warm shelter of hearth and home. In what he described to his publisher as "a homely picture of New England homes," Whittier, who was mourning the death of his sister, makes a statement on the indestructibility of life and love. "Snow-Bound" appeared in book form in February 1866 and was an immediate hit. War-weary Americans, nostalgic for their rural past in the face of the Industrial Revolution, bought up the first print run of 10,000 copies by April.

The sun that brief December day
Rose cheerless over hills of gray,
And, darkly circled, gave at noon
A sadder light than waning moon.
Slow tracing down the thickening sky
Its mute and ominous prophecy,
A portent seeming less than threat,
It sank from sight before it set.
A chill no coat, however stout,
Of homespun stuff could quite shut out,
A hard, dull bitterness of cold,
That checked, mid-vein, the circling race
Of life-blood in the sharpened face,
The coming of the snow-storm told.
The wind blew east; we heard the roar
Of Ocean on his wintry shore,
And felt the strong pulse throbbing there
Beat with low rhythm our inland air.

Meanwhile we did our nightly chores,—
Brought in the wood from out of doors,
Littered the stalls, and from the mows
Raked down the herd's-grass for the cows;
Heard the horse whinnying for his corn;
And, sharply clashing horn on horn,
Impatient down the stanchion rows
The cattle shake their walnut bows;
While, peering from his early perch
Upon the scaffold's pole of birch,
The cock his crested helmet bent
And down his querulous challenge sent.

Unwarmed by any sunset light
The gray day darkened into night,
A night made hoary with the swarm
And whirl-dance of the blinding storm,
As zigzag, wavering to and fro,

Crossed and recrossed the wingëd snow:
And ere the early bedtime came
The white drift piled the window-frame,
And through the glass the clothes-line posts
Looked in like tall and sheeted ghosts.
. . .
As night drew on, and, from the crest
Of wooded knolls that ridged the west,
The sun, a snow-blown traveller, sank
From sight beneath the smothering bank,
We piled, with care, our nightly stack
Of wood against the chimney-back,—
The oaken log, green, huge, and thick,
And on its top the stout back-stick;
The knotty forestick laid apart,
And filled between with curious art
The ragged brush; then, hovering near,
We watched the first red blaze appear,
Heard the sharp crackle, caught the gleam
On whitewashed wall and sagging beam,
Until the old, rude-furnished room
Burst, flower-like, into rosy bloom;
While radiant with a mimic flame
Outside the sparkling drift became,
And through the bare-boughed lilac-tree
Our own warm hearth seemed blazing free.
The crane and pendent trammels showed,
The Turks' heads on the andirons glowed;
While childish fancy, prompt to tell
The meaning of the miracle,
Whispered the old rhyme: "*Under the tree,
When fire outdoors burns merrily,
There the witches are making tea.*"

The moon above the eastern wood
Shone at its full; the hill-range stood
Transfigured in the silver flood,

Its blown snows flashing cold and keen,
Dead white, save where some sharp ravine
Took shadow, or the sombre green
Of hemlocks turned to pitchy black
Against the whiteness at their back.
For such a world and such a night
Most fitting that unwarming light,
Which only seemed where'er it fell
To make the coldness visible.

Source: Poetry Foundation (www.poetryfoundation.org).

Bibliography

Arvin, Newton. *Herman Melville.* New York: Sloan, 1950.

————. *Longfellow: His Life and Work.* Boston: Little, Brown, 1963.

Baker, Carlos. *Emerson Among the Eccentrics: A Group Portrait.* New York: Viking, 1996.

Baym, Nina. *The Norton Anthology of American Literature,* 8th ed. New York: Oxford University Press, 2012.

Bode, Carl. *The American Lyceum: Town Meeting of the Mind.* New York: Oxford University Press, 1956.

Bowden, Mary Weatherspoon. *Washington Irving.* Boston: Twayne, 1981.

Branch, Michael P., ed. *Reading the Roots: American Nature Writing Before Walden.* Athens: University of Georgia Press, 2004.

Brooks, Van Wyck. *The World of Washington Irving.* New York: E.P. Dutton, 1944.

Buell, Lawrence. *Emerson.* Cambridge, MA: Belknap, 2003.

————. *The Environmental Imagination: Thoreau, Nature Writing, and the Formation of American Culture.* Cambridge, MA: Harvard University Press, 1995.

Burstein, Andrew. *The Original Knickerbocker: The Life of Washington Irving.* New York: Basic Books, 2007.

Calhoun, Charles C. *Longfellow: A Rediscovered Life.* Boston: Beacon, 2004.

Capper, Charles. *Margaret Fuller: An American Romantic Life.* New York: Oxford University Press, 1992.

Carpenter, Kenneth E. *Readers and Libraries: Toward a History of Libraries and Culture in America.* Washington, DC: Library of Congress, 1996.

Cheever, Susan. *American Bloomsbury: Louisa May Alcott, Ralph Waldo Emerson, Margaret Fuller, Nathaniel Hawthorne, and Henry David Thoreau; Their Lives, Their Loves, Their Work.* Detroit: Thorndike Press, 2006.

Clark, Robert, ed. *James Fenimore Cooper: New Critical Essays.* Totowa, NJ: Barnes & Noble, 1985.

Davidson, Cathy N. *Revolution and the Word: The Rise of the Novel in America.* New York: Oxford University Press, 1986.

Delbanco, Andrew. *Melville, His World and Work.* New York: Alfred A. Knopf, 2005.

Dickenson, Donna. *Margaret Fuller: Writing a Woman's Life.* New York: St. Martin's Press, 1993.

Duberman, Martin. *James Russell Lowell.* Boston: Beacon, 1966.

Emerson, Ralph Waldo. *Collected Works of Ralph Waldo Emerson.* 6 vols. Edited by Alfred R. Ferguson. Cambridge, MA: Belknap Press, 1971–2003.

Francis, Richard. *Transcendental Utopias: Individual and Community at Brook Farm, Fruitlands, and Walden.* Ithaca, NY: Cornell University Press, 1997.

Frank, Frederick S., and Anthony Magistrale, eds. *The Poe Encyclopedia.* Westport, CT: Greenwood, 1997.

Gado, Frank, ed. *William Cullen Bryant: An American Voice.* Hartford, VT: Antoca, 2006.

Gates, Henry Louis, Jr., ed. *The Classic Slave Narratives.* New York: New American Library, 1987.

Gibbons, Peter. *Oliver Wendell Holmes and the Culture of Conversation.* New York: Cambridge University Press, 2001.

Gura, Philip F. *American Transcendentalism: A History.* New York: Hill and Wang, 2007.

———. *The Crossroads of American History and Literature.* University Park: Pennsylvania State University Press, 1996.

Harding, Walter Roy. *The Days of Henry Thoreau: A Biography.* Princeton, NJ: Princeton University Press, 1982.

Hayes, Kevin J. *The Oxford Handbook of Early American Literature.* New York: Oxford University Press, 2008.

Irmscher, Christoph. *Longfellow Redux.* Urbana: University of Illinois Press, 2006.

Kaser, David. *A Book for a Sixpence: The Circulating Library in America.* Pittsburgh, PA: Beta Phi Mu, 1980.

Kendall, Joshua C. *The Forgotten Founding Father: Noah Webster's Obsession and the Creation of an American Culture.* New York: G.P. Putnam's Sons, 2010.

Kennedy, George, Jr., ed. *A Historical Guide to Edgar Allan Poe.* New York: Oxford University Press, 2001.

Kornfeld, Eve. *Margaret Fuller: A Brief Biography with Documents.* Boston: Bedford, 1997.

Lepore, Jill. *A Is for American: Letters and Other Characters in the Newly United States.* New York: Alfred A. Knopf, 2002.

Long, Robert Emmet. *James Fenimore Cooper.* New York: Continuum, 1990.

Matthiessen, F.O. *American Renaissance: Art and Expression in the Age of Emerson and Whitman.* New York: Oxford University Press, 1941.

McConachie, Bruce A. *Melodramatic Formations: American Theatre and Society, 1820–1870.* Iowa City: University of Iowa Press, 1992.

McFarland, Philip. *Hawthorne in Concord.* New York: Grove, 2005.

Meyers, Jeffrey. *Edgar Allan Poe: His Life and Legacy.* New York: Charles Scribner's Sons, 1992.

Mulford, Carla, Angela Vietto, and Amy E. Winans. *Early American Writings.* New York: Oxford University Press, 2002.

Muller, Gilbert H. *William Cullen Bryant: Author of America.* Albany: State University of New York Press, 2008.

Mumford, Louis. *Herman Melville: A Study of His Life and Vision.* New York: Harcourt, Brace & World, 1962.

Nash, Roderick. *Wilderness and the American Mind.* New Haven, CT: Yale University Press, 2001.

Newman, Lane. *Our Common Dwelling: Henry Thoreau, Transcendentalism, and the Class Politics of Nature.* New York: Palgrave Macmillan, 2005.

Parker, Hershel. *Herman Melville: A Biography.* 2 vols. Baltimore: Johns Hopkins University Press, 1996.

Railton, Stephen. *Fenimore Cooper: A Study of His Life and Imagination.* Princeton, NJ: Princeton University Press, 1978.

Richards, Jeffrey H. *Early American Drama.* New York: Penguin, 1997.

Richardson, Robert D., Jr. *Emerson: The Mind on Fire.* Berkeley: University of California Press, 1995.

———. *Henry Thoreau: A Life of the Mind.* Berkeley: University of California Press, 1986.

Rose, Anne C. *Transcendentalism as a Social Movement, 1830–1850.* New Haven, CT: Yale University Press, 1981.

Schreiner, Samuel A., Jr. *The Concord Quartet: Alcott, Emerson, Hawthorne, Thoreau, and the Friendship That Freed the American Mind.* Hoboken, NJ: John Wiley & Sons, 2006.

Swann, Charles. *Nathaniel Hawthorne: Tradition and Revolution.* New York: Cambridge University Press, 2009.

Tompkins, Jane. *Sensational Designs: The Cultural Work of American Fiction, 1790–1860.* New York: Oxford University Press, 1985.

Unger, Harlow G. *Noah Webster: The Life and Times of an American Patriot.* New York: John Wiley & Sons, 1998.

Wagenknecht, Edward. *James Russell Lowell: Portrait of a Many-Sided Man.* New York: Oxford University Press, 1971.

————. *John Greenleaf Whittier: A Portrait in Paradox.* New York: Oxford University Press, 1967.

Weinstein, Michael A. *The Imaginative Prose of Oliver Wendell Holmes.* Columbia: University of Missouri Press, 2006.

Wineapple, Brenda. *Hawthorne: A Life.* New York: Alfred A. Knopf, 2003.

Woodwell, Roland H. *John Greenleaf Whittier: A Biography.* Haverhill, MA: Trustees of the John Greenleaf Whittier Homestead, 1985.

Ziff, Larzer. *Literary Democracy: The Declaration of Cultural Independence in America.* New York: Penguin, 1982.

————. *Writing in the New Nation: Prose, Print, and Politics in the Early United States.* New Haven, CT: Yale University Press, 1991.

Web Sites

American Transcendentalism Web: http://transcendentalism.tamu.edu

American Verse Project, University of Michigan: http://quod.lib.umich.edu/a/amverse

Archiving Early America: www.earlyamerica.com

Cambridge History of English and American Literature, An Encyclopedia in Eighteen Volumes. Volume XV: Early National Literature, Parts I and II: www.bartleby.com/225/index.html and www.bartleby.com/226/index.html

Early America Review: www.earlyamerica.com/review

Early American Literature (journal): http://earlyamlit.nd.edu

The Edgar Allan Poe Society of Baltimore: www.eapoe.org

Fruitlands Museum: www.fruitlands.org

Hawthorne in Salem, North Shore Community College: www.hawthorneinsalem.org

Henry Wadsworth Longfellow, Maine Historical Society: www.hwlongfellow.org

James Fenimore Cooper Society: http://external.oneonta.edu/cooper

Library of Congress: www.loc.gov

The Melville Society: http://melvillesociety.org

Nineteenth-Century Documents Project: www.furman.edu/~benson/docs

Poets' Corner: www.theotherpages.org/poems

Ralph Waldo Emerson, The Complete Works: www.rwe.org

Sharpe Online Reference: www.sharpe-online.com

Walden Woods Project, Thoreau Institute: www.walden.org

Index